# The Christian Book
## of
## Mystical Verse

*Selected and with an Introduction and Notes by*

## A. W. TOZER

ISBN: 978-1-63923-110-2

Printed: September 2021

Cover Art By: Paul Amid

Published and Distributed By:
Lushena Books
607 Country Club Drive, Unit E
Bensenville, IL 60106
www.lushenabks.com

ISBN: 978-1-63923-110-2

Printed in the United States of America

p

# The Christian Book
## of
# Mystical Verse

*Selected and with an Introduction and Notes by*

## A. W. TOZER

**CHRISTIAN PUBLICATIONS, INC.**

25 So. Tenth St.,     Harrisburg, Pa. 17101

# INTRODUCTION

The purpose of this book is to bring together in one convenient volume some of the best devotional verse the English language affords, and thus to make available to present day Christians a rich spiritual heritage which the greater number of them for various reasons do not now enjoy.

I have not hesitated to apply the term "mystical" to the material I have collected here, though I readily admit that fewer than half a dozen of the men and women who would be called true mystics in the strict classical sense will be found here. Such names as Eckhart, Ruysbroeck, John of the Cross, Teresa, Rolle, Tauler, Hilton, Francis of Assisi, for instance, are not represented in this volume at all. On the other hand the frequent appearance of such a man as Watts might cause the reader to lift a questioning eyebrow and ask, "Is Watts also among the mystics?"

Well, the answer must be, Of course he is, and so are John Newton and James Montgomery and Reginald Heber and Charles Wesley, as well as many others who might have balked at being called mystics but whose writings, nevertheless, reveal unmistakable traces of purest mysticism and are the better for it. And for that matter the same thing may be said of the inspired writings of such men as Moses and David and Isaiah and Daniel and Paul and John, the works of the latter showing more than traces of the mystical spirit, being indeed charged full with it.

As short a time as, say, forty years ago, the words "mystic" and "mystical" were altogether unacceptable in evangelical circles. Among the gospel churches the words suggested someone who was emotionally unstable, visionary, and worst of all, unsound theologically.

Now there are undoubtedly many persons with a temperamental fondness for the fantastic. These have by nature a strong psychic bent that predisposes them toward the occult; they have also an incredible capacity for self-deception and are ready to accept whatever in the realm of religion is bizarre and prodigious. Such as these have been sometimes called mystics—something they most surely are not.

The word "mystic" as it occurs in the title of this book refers to that personal spiritual experience common to the saints of Bible times and well known to multitudes of persons in the post-Biblical era. I refer to the evangelical mystic who has been brought by the gospel into intimate fellowship with the Godhead. His theology is no less and no more than is taught in the Christian Scriptures. He walks the high road of truth where walked of old prophets and apostles, and where down the centuries walked martyrs, reformers, Puritans, evangelists and missionaires of the cross. He differs from the ordinary orthodox Christian only because he experiences his faith down in the depths of his sentient being while the other does not. He exists in a world of spiritual reality. He is quietly, deeply, and sometimes almost ecstatically aware of the Presence of God in his own nature and in the world around him. His religious experience is something elemental, as old as time and the creation. It is immediate acquaintance with God by union with the Eternal Son. It is to know that which passes knowledge.

The hymns and poems found here are mystical in that they are God-oriented; they begin with God, embrace the worshipping soul and return to God again. And they cover almost the full spectrum of religious feeling: fear, hope, penitence, aspiration, the longing to be holy, yearning after God, gratitude, thanksgiving, pure admiration of the Godhead, love for Christ, worship, praise and adoration. The mood runs from near despair to near ecstasy, and the twin notes of utter sincerity and deepest reverence may be heard throughout.

This is a book for the worshiper rather than for the student. It has been carefully and lovingly prepared for those God-enamored persons who, while they feel as deeply as the enraptured poet, yet lack the gift that would enable them to express their feelings adequately. Such will sense a kinship with the gifted souls they find on the pages of this book and will join them as they mount on high to pour out their hymns at heaven's gate.

In making these selections I have largely followed my own bent, though I have been guided somewhat by a few simple rules. First, all sentimental verse was excluded, along with everything homey and maudlin. The only healthy emotions are those aroused by great ideas, and even these must be restrained and purified by the Spirit of God or they will spend themselves in weak and sterile rhymes. Of such there is enough in the religious world; I think none will be found in this book.

Second, while the compiler is not unfamiliar with the judgment of hymnologists and literary critics on the larger body of English religious verse, that judgment has been set aside and another adopted for this book. For this reason some of the standard classics have been omitted because I felt they would not contribute to my purpose. Conversely, certain poems of admittedly inferior literary rank have been included because I felt that they would.

Third, everything selected for inclusion in this work had to be judged theologically sound. While considerable latitude was allowed, even welcomed, in doctrinal outlook and emphasis, to be accepted every hymn and poem had to meet the test of faithfulness to the Christian Scriptures.

Though almost everything here is pure lyric poetry and may easily be sung, yet this book is not intended for use in the public assembly. Had I meant it to be so used a wholly different kind of verse would have been chosen for it and the book would have been another sort of book altogether. Everything here is for use in private devotion. I have had in mind not a congregation but the lone individual. For this reason I would respectfully urge the one who may come into possession of this book not to "read" it as he would read another book. Let him try rather to enter into its mood, to capture and be captured by its spirit. How many pages he gets through in a day is of no importance; what one poem or even one single stanza does to him and for him and in him: that is everything.

Admittedly much pure gold has been left out of this treasury. The chief reason is lack of space. I have tried to keep the book small enough to be portable, that its possessor may carry it with him and so turn any bus or train or airplane into a sanctuary. Certainly not all the gold in the world is in this one volume, but what is here is, I believe, true gold of Ophir. I hope many of my fellow Christians will find it to be so.

A. W. Tozer

# CONTENTS

# Adoration of the Godhead

Eternal Power, whose high abode
Becomes the grandeur of a God:
Infinite lengths beyond the bounds
Where stars revolve their little rounds:

Thee while the first archangel sings,
He hides his face behind his wings:
And ranks of shining thrones around
Fall worshipping, and spread the ground.

Lord, what shall earth and ashes do?
We would adore our Maker too;
From sin and dust to Thee we cry,
The Great, the Holy, and the High.

Earth, from afar, hath heard Thy fame,
And worms have learn'd to lisp Thy Name;
But O! the glories of Thy mind
Leave all our soaring thoughts behind.

God is in heaven, and men below:
Be short our tunes; our words be few:
A solemn reverence checks our songs,
And praise sits silent on our tongues.

—Isaac Watts, 1674-1748

# ¶ LORD OF ALL BEING

Lord of all being, throned afar,
Thy glory flames from sun and star;
Center and soul of every sphere,
Yet to each loving heart how near.

Sun of our life, Thy quickening ray
Sheds on our path the glow of day;
Star of our hope, Thy softened light
Cheers the long watches of the night.

Our midnight is Thy smile withdrawn;
Our noontide is Thy gracious dawn;
Our rainbow arch, Thy mercy's sign;
All, save the clouds of sin, are Thine.

Lord of all life, below, above,
Whose light is truth, whose warmth is love,
Before Thy ever blazing throne
We ask no luster of our own.

Grant us Thy truth to make us free,
And kindling hearts that burn for Thee,
Till all Thy living altars claim
One holy light, one heavenly flame.

—OLIVER WENDELL HOLMES, 1809-1894


# ¶ ADORATION

Almighty One! I bend in dust before Thee;
    Even so veiled cherubs bend;
In calm and still devotion I adore Thee,
    All-wise, all-present Friend!

2

Thou to the earth its emerald robes hast given,
　　Or curtained it in snow;
And the bright sun, and the soft moon in heaven,
　　Before Thy presence bow.

Thou Power sublime! whose throne is firmly seated
　　On stars and glowing suns;
O, could I praise Thee,—could my soul, elated,
　　Waft Thee seraphic tones, —
Had I the lyres of angels, —could I bring Thee
　　An offering worthy Thee, —
In what bright notes of glory would I sing Thee,
　　Blest notes of ecstasy!

Eternity! Eternity! how solemn,
　　How terrible the sound!
Here, leaning on thy promises, —a column
　　Of strength, —may I be found,
O, let my heart be ever Thine, while beating,
　　As when 'twill cease to beat!
Be Thou my portion, till that awful meeting
　　When I my God shall greet!

　　　　　　　—Sir John Bowring, 1792-1872


## ¶ THE UNITY OF GOD

One God! one Majesty!
There is no God but Thee!
Unbounded, unextended Unity!

Awful in unity,
O God! we worship Thee,
More simply one, because supremely Three!

Dread, unbeginning One!
Single, yet not alone,
Creation hath not set Thee on a higher throne.

3

Unfathomable Sea!
All life is out of Thee,
And Thy life is Thy blissful Unity.

All things that from Thee run,
All works that Thou hast done,
Thou didst in honour of Thy being One.

And by Thy being One,
Ever by that alone,
Couldst Thou do, and doest, what Thou hast done.

We from Thy oneness come,
Beyond it cannot roam,
And in Thy oneness find our one eternal home.

Blest be Thy Unity!
All joys are one to me,—
The joy that there can be no other God than Thee!

—FREDERICK WILLIAM FABER, 1814-1863


¶ THE HOLY TRINITY

O Blessed Trinity!
Thy children dare to lift their hearts to Thee,
And bless Thy triple Majesty!
Holy Trinity!
Blessed Equal Three,
One God, we praise Thee.

O Blessed Trinity!
Holy, unfathomable, infinite,
Thou art all Life and Love and Light.
Holy Trinity!
Blessed Equal Three,
One God, we praise Thee.

4

O Blessed Trinity!
God of a thousand attributes! we see
     That there is no one good but Thee.
          Holy Trinity!
          Blessed Equal Three,
          One God, we praise Thee.


O Blessed Trinity!
In our astonished reverence we confess
     Thine uncreated loveliness.
          Holy Trinity!
          Blessed Equal Three,
          One God, we praise Thee.


O Blessed Trinity!
O simplest Majesty! O Three in One!
     Thou art for ever God alone.
          Holy Trinity!
          Blessed Equal Three,
          One God, we praise Thee.


O Blessed Trinity!
The Fountain of the Godhead, in repose,
     For ever rests, for ever flows.
          Holy Trinity!
          Blessed Equal Three,
          One God, we praise Thee.


O Blessed Trinity!
O Unbegotten Father! give us tears
     To quench our love, to calm our fears.
          Holy Trinity!
          Blessed Equal Three,
          One God, we praise Thee.

O Blessed Trinity!
Bright Son! who art the Father's mind displayed,
    Thou art begotten and not made.
        Holy Trinity!
        Blessed Equal Three,
        One God, we praise Thee.


O Blessed Trinity!
Coequal Spirit! wondrous Paraclete!
    By Thee the Godhead is complete.
        Holy Trinity!
        Blessed Equal Three,
        One God, we praise Thee.


O Blessed Trinity!
We praise Thee, bless Thee, worship Thee as one.
    Yet Three are on the single Throne.
        Holy Trinity!
        Blessed Equal Three,
        One God, we praise Thee.


O Blessed Trinity!
In the deep darkness of prayer's stillest night
    We worship Thee blinded with light.
        Holy Trinity!
        Blessed Equal Three,
        One God, we praise Thee.


O Blessed Trinity!
Oh would that we could die of love for Thee,
    Incomparable Trinity!
        Holy Trinity!
        Blessed Equal Three,
        One God, we praise Thee.

—FREDERICK WILLIAM FABER, 1814-1863

# ¶ MAJESTY DIVINE!

Full of glory, full of wonders,
  Majesty Divine!
Mid Thine everlasting thunders
  How Thy lightnings shine!
Shoreless Ocean! who shall sound Thee?
Thine own eternity is round Thee,
  Majesty Divine!

Timeless, spaceless, single, lonely,
  Yet sublimely Three,
Thou art grandly, always, only
  God in Unity!
Lone in grandeur, lone in glory,
Who shall tell Thy wondrous story,
  Awful Trinity?

Speechlessly, without beginning,
  Sun that never rose!
Vast, adorable, and winning,
  Day that hath no close!
Bliss from Thine own glory tasting,
Everliving, everlasting,
  Life that never grows!

Thine own Self for ever filling
  With self-kindled flame,
In Thyself Thou art distilling
  Unctions without name!
Without worshipping of creatures
Without veiling of Thy features,
  God always the same!

In Thy praise of Self untiring
  Thy perfections shine;
Self-sufficient, self-admiring,—
  Such life must be Thine;—

Glorifying Self, yet blameless
With a sanctity all shameless
    It is so divine!

'Mid Thine uncreated morning,
    Like a trembling star
I behold creation's dawning
    Glimmering from afar;
Nothing giving, nothing taking,
Nothing changing, nothing breaking,
    Waiting at time's bar!

I with life and love diurnal
    See myself in Thee,
All embalmed in love eternal,
    Floating in Thy sea:
'Mid Thine uncreated whiteness
I behold Thy glory's brightness
    Feed itself on me.

Splendours upon splendours beaming
    Change and intertwine;
Glories over glories streaming
    All translucent shine!
Blessings, praises adorations
Greet Thee from the trembling nations
    Majesty Divine!

—Frederick William Faber, 1814-1863

## ¶ THE VISION OF THE GODHEAD

Unchanging and Unchangeable, before angelic
    eyes,
The Vision of the Godhead in its tranquil
    beauty lies;

8

And, like a city lighted up all gloriously within,
Its countless lustres glance and gleam, and
    sweetest worship win.
On the Unbegotten Father, awful well-spring
    of the Three,
On the Sole Begotten Son's coequal Majesty.
On Him eternally breathed forth from Father
    and from Son.
The spirits gaze with fixed amaze, and unreck-
    oned ages run.


Chorus:

Myriad, myriad angels raise
Happy hymns of wondering praise,
    Ever through eternal days,
    Before the Holy Trinity,
    One Undivided Three!


Still the Fountain of the Godhead giveth forth
    eternal being:
Still begetting, unbegotten, still His own per-
    fection seeing,
Still limiting His own loved Self with His
    dear coequal Spirit,
No change comes o'er that blissful Life, no
    shadow passeth near it.
And beautiful dread Attributes, all manifold
    and bright,
Now thousands seem, now lose themselves in
    one self-living light;
And far in that deep Life of God, in harmony
    complete,
Like crowned kings, all opposite perfections
    take their seat.
And in that ungrowing vision nothing deep-
    ens, nothing brightens,
But the living Life of God perpetually lightens;

9

And created life is nothing but a radiant shad-
　　ow fleeing
From the unapproached lustres of that Unbe-
　　ginning Being;
Spirits wise and deep have watched that ever-
　　lasting Ocean,
And never o'er its lucid field hath rippled
　　faintest motion;
In glory undistinguished never have the Three
　　seemed One,
Nor ever in divided streams the Single Es-
　　sence run.

There reigns the Eternal Father, in His lone
　　prerogatives,
And, in the Father's Mind, the Son, all self-
　　existing, lives,
With Him, their mutual Jubilee, that deepest
　　depth of love,
Lifegiving Life of two-fold source, the many
　　gifted Dove!
O Bountiful! O Beautiful! can Power or Wis-
　　dom add
Fresh features to a life, so munificent and
　　glad?
Can even uncreated Love, ye angels! give a
　　hue
Which can ever make the Unchanging and
　　Unchangeable look new?

The Mercy of the Merciful is equal to Their
　　Might,
As wondrous as Their Love, and as Their
　　Wisdom bright!
As They, who out of nothing called creation
　　at the first,
In everlasting purposes Their own design had
　　nursed,—

As They, who in their solitude, Three Per-
    sons, once abode,
Vouchsafed of Their abundance to become
    creation's God,—
What They owed not to Themselves They
    stooped to owe to man,
And pledged Their glory to him, in an unim-
    aginable plan.


See! deep within the glowing depth of that
    Eternal Light.
What change hath come, what vision new
    transports angelic sight?
A creature can it be, in uncreated bliss?
A novelty in God? Oh what nameless thing
    is this?
The beauty of the Father's Power is o'er it
    brightly shed,
The sweetness of the Spirit's Love is unction
    on its head;
In the wisdom of the Son it plays its won-
    drous part,
While it lives the loving life of a real Human
    heart!


A Heart that hath a Mother, and a treasure of
    red blood,
A Heart that man can pray to, and feed upon
    for food!
In the brightness of the Godhead is its marvellous
    abode,
A change in the Unchanging, creation touching
    God!
Ye spirits blest, in endless rest, who on that
    Vision gaze,
Salute the Sacred Heart with all your worship-
    ful amaze,

And adore, while with ecstatic skill the Three
  in One ye scan,
The Mercy that hath planted there that blessed Heart of Man!


All tranquilly, all tranquilly, doth that Blissful
  Vision last,
And Its brightness o'er immortalized creation
  will it cast;
Ungrowing and unfading, Its pure Essence
  doth it keep,
In the deepest of those depths where all are
    infinitely deep;
Unchanging and Unchangeable as It hath ever been,
As It was before that Human heart was there
  by angels seen,
So is it at this very hour, so will it ever be,
With that Human Heart within It, beating hot
  with love of me!

Chorus:

Myriad, myriad angels raise
Happy hymns of wondering praise,
Ever through eternal days,
  Before the Holy Trinity,
  One Undivided Three!

—FREDERICK WILLIAM FABER, 1814-1863



¶ THE THOUGHT OF GOD

The thought of God, the thought of Thee,
  Who liest in my heart,
And yet beyond imagined space
  Outstretched and present art,—

12

The thought of Thee, above, below,
  Around me and within,
Is more to me than health and wealth,
  Or love of kith and kin.

The thought of God is like the tree
  Beneath whose shade I lie,
And watch the fleets of snowy clouds
  Sail o'er the silent sky.

'Tis like that soft invading light,
  Which in all darkness shines,
The thread that through life's sombre web
  In golden pattern twines.

It is a thought which ever makes
  Life's sweetest smiles from tears,
And is a daybreak to our hopes,
  A sunset to our fears;

One while it bids the tears to flow,
  Then wipes them from the eyes,
Most often fills our souls with joy,
  And always sanctifies.

Within a thought so great, our souls
  Little and modest grow,
And, by its vastness awed, we learn
  The art of walking slow.

The wild flower on the mossy ground
  Scarce bends its pliant form,
When overhead the autumnal wood
  Is thundering like a storm.

So is it with our humbled souls
  Down in the thought of God,
Scarce conscious in their sober peace
  Of the wild storms abroad.

To think of Thee is almost prayer,
　　And is outspoken praise;
And pain can even passive thoughts
　　To actual worship raise.

O Lord! I live always in pain,
　　My life's sad undersong,
Pain in itself not hard to bear,
　　But hard to bear so long.

Little sometimes weighs more than much,
　　When it has no relief;
A joyless life is worse to bear
　　Than one of active grief.

And yet, O Lord! a suffering life
　　One grand ascent may dare;
Penance, not self-imposed, can make
　　The whole of life a prayer.

All murmurs lie inside Thy Will
　　Which are to Thee addressed;
To suffer for Thee is our work,
　　To think of Thee our rest.

　　　　—FREDERICK WILLIAM FABER, 1814-1863

## ¶ THE GREATNESS OF GOD

O Majesty unspeakable and dread!
　　Wert Thou less mighty than Thou art,
Thou wert, O Lord! too great for our belief,
　　Too little for our heart.

Thy greatness would seem monstrous by the side
　　Of creatures frail and undivine;
Yet they would have a greatness of their own
　　Free and apart from Thine.

Such grandeur were but a created thing,
  A spectre, terror, and a grief,
Out of all keeping with a world so calm,
  Oppressing our belief.

But greatness, which is infinite makes room
  For all things in its lap to lie;
We should be crushed by a magnificence
  Short of infinity.

It would outgrow us from the face of things,
  Still prospering as we decayed,
And, like a tyrannous rival, it would feed
  Upon the wrecks it made.

But what is infinite must be a home,
  A shelter for the meanest life,
Where it is free to reach its greatest growth
  Far from the touch of strife.

We share in what is infinite: 'tis ours,
  For we and it alike are Thine;
What I enjoy, great God! by right of Thee
  Is more than doubly mine.

Thus doth Thy hospitable greatness lie
  Outside us like a boundless sea;
We cannot lose ourselves where all is home,
  Nor drift away from Thee.

Out on that sea we are in harbour still,
  And scarce advert to winds and tides,
Like ships that ride at anchor, with the waves
  Flapping against their sides.

Thus doth Thy grandeur make us grand ourselves;
  'Tis goodness bids us fear;
Thy greatness makes us brave as children are,
  When those they love are near.

15

Great God, our lowliness takes heart to play
　　Beneath the shadow of Thy state;
The only comfort of our littleness
　　Is that Thou art so great.

Then on Thy grandeur I will lay me down;
　　Already life is heaven for me;
No cradled child more softly lies than I,—
　　Come soon, Eternity!

　　　　　—FREDERICK WILLIAM FABER, 1814-1863


## ¶ THE ETERNITY OF GOD

　　　　O Lord! my heart is sick,
　　Sick of this everlasting change;
　　　　And life runs tediously quick
　　Through its unresting race and varied range:
　Change finds no likeness to itself in Thee,
And wakes no echo in Thy mute Eternity.

　　　　Dear Lord! my heart is sick
　　Of this perpetual lapsing time,
　　　　So slow in grief, in joy so quick,
　　Yet ever casting shadows so sublime;
　Time of all creatures is least like to Thee,
And yet it is our share of Thine eternity.

　　　　O change and time are storms
　　For lives so thin and frail as ours;
　　　　For change the work of grace deforms
　　With love that soils, and help that overpowers;
　And time is strong, and, like some chafing sea,
It seems to fret the shores of Thine eternity.

16

Weak, weak, forever weak!
We cannot hold what we possess;
    Youth cannot find, age will not seek,
O weakness is the heart's worst weariness:
But weakest hearts can lift their thoughts to Thee;
It makes us strong to think of Thine eternity.


Thou hadst no youth, great God,
An Unbeginning End Thou art;
    Thy glory in itself abode,
And still abides in its own tranquil heart:
No age can heap its outward years on Thee:
Dear God! Thou art Thyself Thine own eternity!


Without an end or bound
Thy life lies all outspread in light;
    Our lives feel Thy life all around,
Making our weakness strong, our darkness bright;
Yet is it neither wilderness nor sea,
But the calm gladness of a full eternity.


Oh Thou art very great
To set Thyself so far above!
    But we partake of Thine estate,
Established in Thy strength and in Thy love:
That love hath made eternal room for me
In the sweet vastness of its own eternity.


Oh Thou art very meek
To overshade Thy creatures thus!
    Thy grandeur is the shade we seek:
To be eternal is Thy use to us:
Ah Blessed God! what joy it is to me
To lose all thought of self in Thine eternity.


Self-wearied, Lord! I come;
For I have lived my life too fast:
    Now that years bring me nearer home

Grace must be slowly used to make it last;
   When my heart beats too quick I think of Thee,
And of the leisure of Thy long eternity.

   Farewell, vain joys of earth!
Farewell, all love that is not His!
   Dear God! be Thou my only mirth,
Thy majesty my single timid bliss!
Oh in the bosom of eternity
Thou does not weary of Thyself, nor we of Thee!

—Frederick William Faber, 1814-1863


¶ THE FEAR OF GOD

My fear of Thee, O Lord, exults
   Like life within my veins,
A fear which rightly claims to be
   One of love's sacred pains.

Thy goodness to Thy saints of old
   An awful thing appeared;
For were Thy majesty less good
   Much less would it be feared.

There is no joy the soul can meet
   Upon life's various road
Like the sweet fear that sits and shrinks
   Under the eye of God.

A special joy is in all love
   For objects we revere;
Thus joy in God will always be
   Proportioned to our fear.

Oh Thou art greatly to be feared,
   Thou art so prompt to bless!
The dread to miss such love as Thine
   Makes fear but love's excess.

18

The fulness of Thy mercy seems
  To fill both land and sea;
If we can break through bounds so vast,
  How exiled shall we be!

For grace is fearful, which each hour
  Our path in life has crossed;
If it were rarer, it might be
  Less easy to be lost.

But fear is love, and love is fear,
  And in and out they move;
But fear is an intenser joy
  Than mere unfrightened love.

When most I fear Thee, Lord! then most
  Familiar I appear;
And I am in my soul most free,
  When I am most in fear.

I should not love Thee as I do,
  If love might make more free;
Its very sweetness would be lost
  In greater liberty.

I feel Thee most a father, when
  I fancy Thee most near:
And Thou comest not so nigh in love
  As Thou comest, Lord! in fear.

They love Thee little, if at all,
  Who do not fear Thee much;
If love is Thine attraction, Lord!
  Fear is Thy very touch.

Love could not love Thee half so much
  If it found Thee not so near;
It is thy nearness, which makes love
  The perfectness of fear.

We fear because Thou art so good,
  And because we can sin;
And when we make most show of love,
  We are trembling most within.

And Father! when to us in heaven
  Thou shalt Thy Face unveil,
Then more than ever will our souls
  Before Thy goodness quail.

Our blessedness will be to bear
  The sight of Thee so near,
And thus eternal love will be
  But the ecstasy of fear.

—Frederick William Faber, 1814-1863


¶ THE ETERNAL FATHER

Father! the sweetest, dearest Name.
  That men or angels know!
Fountain of life, that had no fount
  From which itself could flow!

Thy life is one unwearing day;
  Before its Now Thou hast
No varied future yet unlived,
  No lapse of changeless past.

Thou comest not, Thou goest not;
  Thou wert not, wilt not be;
Eternity is but a thought
  By which we think of Thee.

No epochs lie behind Thy life;
  Thou holdst Thy life of none:
No other life is by Thy side;
  Thine is supremely lone.

20

Far upward in the timeless past,
  Ere form or space had come,
We see Thee by Thine own dread light,
  Thyself Thine only home.

Thy vastness is not young or old;
  Thy life hath never grown;
No time can measure out Thy days.
  No space can make Thy throne.

Thy life is deep within Thyself,
  Sole Unbegotten Sire!
But Son and Spirit flow from Thee
  In coeternal fire.

They flow from Thee, They rest in Thee,
  As in a Father's Breast,—
Processions of eternal love,
  Pulses of eternal rest!

That They in majesty should reign
  Coequal, Sire! with Thee,
But magnifies the singleness
  Of Thy paternity.

Their uncreated glories, Lord!
  With Thine own glory shine;
Thy glory as the Father needs
  That Theirs should equal Thine.

All things are equal in Thy life:
  Thou joyst to be alone,
To have no sire, and yet to have
  A coeternal Son.

Thy Spirit is Thy jubilee;
  Thy Word is Thy delight;
Thou givest Them to equal Thee
  In glory and in might.

Thou art too great to keep unshared
  Thy grand eternity;
They have it as Thy gift to Them,
  Which is no gift to Thee.

We too, like Thy coequal Word,
  Within Thy lap may rest:
We too, like Thine Eternal Dove,
  May nestle in Thy Breast.

Lone Fountain of the Godhead! hail!
  Person most dread and dear!
I thrill with frightened joy to feel
  Thy fatherhood so near.

Lost in Thy greatness, Lord! I live,
  As in some gorgeous maze;
Thy sea of unbegotten light
  Blinds me, and yet I gaze.

For Thy grandeur is all tenderness,
  All motherlike and meek;
The hearts that will not come to it
  Humbling itself to seek.

Thou feign'st to be remote, and speakst
  As if from far above,
That fear may make more bold with Thee
  And be beguiled to love.

On earth Thou hidest, not to scare
  The children with Thy light,
Then showest us Thy Face in heaven,
  When we can bear the sight.

All fathers learn their craft from Thee;
  All loves are shadows cast
From the beautiful eternal hills
  Of Thine unbeginning past.

—FREDERICK WILLIAM FABER, 1814-1863

Amid the eternal silences
  God's endless Word was spoken;
None heard but He who always spake,
  And the silence was unbroken.

Chorus.

Oh marvellous! Oh worshipful!
  No song or sound is heard,
But everywhere and every hour,
In love, in wisdom, and in power,
The Father speaks His dear Eternal Word.

For ever in the eternal land
  The glorious day is dawning;
For ever is the Father's Light
  Like an endless outspread morning.

From the Father's vast tranquillity,
  In light coequal glowing
The kingly consubstantial Word
  Is unutterably flowing.

For ever climbs that Morning Star
  Without ascent or motion;
For ever is its daybreak shed
  On the Spirit's boundless ocean.

O Word! who fitly can adore
  Thy Birth and Thy Relation,
Lost in the impenetrable light
  Of Thine awful Generation?

Thy Father clasps Thee evermore
  In unspeakable embraces,
While angels tremble as they praise,
  And shroud their dazzled faces.

And oh! in what abyss of love,
  So fiery yet so tender,
The Holy Ghost encircles Thee
  With His uncreated splendour!

O Word! O dear and gentle Word!
  Thy creatures kneel before Thee,
And in ecstacies of timid love
  Delightedly adore Thee.

Hail choicest mystery of God!
  Hail wondrous Generation!
The Father's self-sufficient rest!
  The Spirit's jubilation!

Dear Person! dear beyond all words,
  Glorious beyond all telling!
Oh with what songs of silent love
  Our ravished hearts are swelling!

Chorus.

O! marvellous! O worshipful!
  No song or sound is heard,
But everywhere and every hour,
In love, in wisdom, and in power,
The Father speaks His dear Eternal Word.

—FREDERICK WILLIAM FABER, 1814-1863

¶ THE HOLY SPIRIT

Fountain of Love! Thyself true God!
  Who through eternal days
From Father and from Son hast flowed
  In uncreated ways!

24

O Majesty unspeakable!
  O Person all divine!
How in the Threefold Majesty
  Doth Thy Procession shine!

Fixed in the Godhead's awful light
  Thy fiery Breath doth move;
Thou art a wonder by Thyself
  To worship and to love!

Proceeding, yet of equal age
  With those whose love Thou art:
Proceeding, yet distinct, from those
  From whom Thou seem'st to part.

And undivided Nature shared
  With Father and with Son;
A Person by Thyself; with Them
  Thy simple essence One;

Bond art Thou of the other Twain!
  Omnipotent and free!
The consummating Love of God!
  The Limit of the Three!

Thou limitest infinity,
  Thyself all infinite;
The Godhead lives, and loves, and rests,
  In Thine eternal light.

I dread Thee, Unbegotten Love!
  True God! sole Fount of Grace!
And now before Thy Blessed throne
  My sinful self abase.

Ocean, wide-flowing Ocean, Thou,
  Of uncreated Love;
I tremble as within my soul
  I feel Thy waters move.

Thou art a sea without a shore;
  Awful, immense Thou art;
A sea which can contract itself
  Within my narrow heart.

And yet Thou art a haven too
  Out on the shoreless sea,
A harbor that can hold full well
  Shipwrecked Humanity.

Thou art an unborn Breath outbreathed
  On angels and on men,
Subduing all things to Thyself,
  We know not how or when.

Thou art a God of fire, that doth
  Create while He consumes!
A God of light, whose rays on earth
  Darken where He illumes!

All things! dread Spirit! to Thy praise
  Thy Presence doth transmute;
Evil itself Thy glory bears,
  Its one abiding fruit!

O Light! O Love! O very God
  I dare no longer gaze
Upon Thy wondrous attributes,
  And their mysterious ways.

O Spirit, beautiful and dread!
  My heart is fit to break
With love of all Thy tenderness
  For us poor sinners' sake.

Thy love of Jesus I adore;
  My comfort this shall be,
That, when I serve my dearest Lord,
  That service worships Thee!

—Frederick William Faber, 1814-1863

26

# ¶ PENTECOST

He comes! He comes! that mighty Breath
  From heaven's eternal shores;
His uncreated freshness fills
  His bride as she adores.

Earth quakes before that rushing blast,
  Heaven echoes back the sound,
And mightily the tempest wheels
  That Upper Room around.

One moment—and the silentness
  Was breathless as the grave;
The fluttered earth forgot to quake,
  The troubled trees to wave.

One moment—and the Spirit hung
  O'er them with dread desire;
Then broke upon the heads of all
  In cloven tongues of fire.

What gifts He gave those chosen men
  Past ages can display;
Nay more, their vigour still inspires
  The weakness of today.

Those tongues still speak within the Church,
  That Fire is undecayed;
Its well-spring was that Upper Room,
  Where the disciples met and prayed.

The Spirit came into the Church
  With His unfailing power;
He is the Living Heart that beats
  Within her at this hour.

Speak gently then of Church and Saints,
    Lest you His ways reprove;
The Heat, the Pulses of the Church
    Are God's Eternal Love.

Oh let us fall and worship Him,
    The Love of Sire and Son,
The Consubstantial Breath of God,
    The Coeternal One!

Ah! see, how like the Incarnate Word,
    His Blessed Self He lowers,
To dwell with us invisibly,
    And make His riches ours.

Most tender Spirit! Mighty God!
    Sweet must Thy Presence be,
If loss of Jesus can be gain,
    So long as we have Thee!

—FREDERICK WILLIAM FABER, 1814-1863

# Devotional Meditations on the Cross of Christ

¶ SWEET THE MOMENTS, RICH IN BLESSING

Sweet the moments, rich in blessing,
    Which before the Cross I spend;
Life and health and peace possessing
    From the sinner's dying Friend.

Truly blessed is this station,
    Low before His Cross to lie;
While I see divine compassion
    Beaming in His languid eye.

Love and grief my heart dividing,
    With my tears His feet I'll bathe;
Constant still in faith abiding,
    Life deriving from His death.

For Thy sorrows we adore Thee—
    For the griefs that wrought our peace—
Gracious Saviour! we implore Thee,
    In our hearts Thy love increase.

—WALTER SHIRLEY *et al.*, 1725-1786

# ¶ RIDE ON! RIDE ON IN MAJESTY!

Ride on! ride on in majesty!
Ride on! ride on in majesty!
Hark! all the tribes "Hosanna" cry:
O Saviour meek, pursue Thy road
With palms and scattered garments strowed.

Ride on! ride on in majesty!
In lowly pomp ride on to die:
O Christ, Thy triumphs now begin
O'er captive death and conquered sin.

Ride on! ride on in majesty!
The winged squadrons of the sky
Look down with sad and wondering eyes
To see the approaching sacrifice.

Ride on! Ride on in majesty!
Thy last and fiercest strife is nigh;
The Father on His sapphire throne
Awaits His own anointed Son.

Ride on! ride on in majesty!
In lowly pomp ride on to die;
Bow Thy meek head to mortal pain,
Then take, O God, Thy power and reign.

—HENRY HART MILMAN, 1791-1868


# ¶ WOULD JESUS HAVE THE SINNER DIE?

Would Jesus have the sinner die?
　　Why hangs He then on yonder tree?
What means that strange expiring cry?
　　(Sinners, He prays for you and me;)
Forgive them, Father, O forgive!
They know not that by Me they live.

Jesus, descended from above,
   Our loss of Eden to retrieve,
Great God of universal love,
   If all the world through Thee may live,
In us a quick'ning spirit be,
And witness Thou hast died for me.

Thou loving, all-atoning Lamb, —
   Thee, by Thy painful agony,
Thy bloody sweat, Thy grief and shame,
   Thy cross and passion on the tree,
Thy precious death and life—I pray,
Take all, take all my sins away.

O let Thy love my heart constrain, —
   Thy love, for every sinner free, —
That every fallen son of man
   May taste the grace that found out me;
That all mankind with me may prove
Thy sov'reign, everlasting love.

—CHARLES WESLEY, 1707-1767


## ¶ HE DIES! THE FRIEND OF SINNERS DIES!

He dies! the Friend of sinners dies!
   Lo! Salem's daughters weep around;
A solemn darkness veils the skies,
   A sudden trembling shakes the ground:
Come, saints, and drop a tear or two
   For Him who groan'd beneath your load;
He shed a thousand drops for you, —
   A thousand drops of richer blood.

Here's love and grief beyond degree:
   The Lord of glory dies for man!
But lo! what sudden joys we see:
   Jesus, the dead, revives again.

31

The rising God forsakes the tomb;
  (In vain the tomb forbids His rise;)
Cherubic legions guard Him home,
  And shout Him welcome to the skies.

Break off your tears, ye saints, and tell
  How high your great Deliv'rer reigns;
Sing how He spoil'd the hosts of hell,
  And led the monster death in chains:
Say, Live forever, wondrous King!
  Born to redeem, and strong to save;
Then ask the monster, Where's thy sting?
  And, Where's thy vict'ry, boasting grave?

—ISAAC WATTS, 1674-1748


## ¶ BEFORE THE CROSS

My Lord, my Master, at Thy feet adoring,
  I see Thee bowed beneath Thy load of woe:
For me, a sinner, is Thy life-blood pouring;
  For Thee, my Saviour, scarce my tears
    will flow.

Thine own disciple to the Jews has sold Thee,
  With friendship's kiss and loyal word he
      came;
How oft of faithful love my lips have told Thee,
  While Thou hast seen my falsehood and my
      shame!

With taunts and scoffs they mock what seems
      Thy weakness,
  With blows and outrage adding pain to pain;
Thou art unmoved and steadfast in Thy meek-
      ness;
  When I am wronged how quickly I complain!

My Lord, my Saviour, when I see Thee wear-
    ing
Upon Thy bleeding brow the crown of thorn,
Shall I for pleasure live, or shrink from bear-
    ing
Whate'er my lot may be of pain or scorn?

O Victim of Thy love, O pangs most healing,
  O saving death, O wounds that I adore,
O shame most glorious! Christ, before Thee
    kneeling,
  I pray Thee keep me Thine for evermore.

—From the French of JACQUES BRIDAINE,
    1701-1767
  *Tr.* THOMAS BENSON POLLOCK, 1836-1896

## ¶ O SACRED HEAD, NOW WOUNDED

O Sacred Head, now wounded,
  With grief and shame weighed down,
Now scornfully surrounded
  With thorns, Thine only crown;
O sacred Head, what glory,
  What bliss, till now was Thine!
Yet though despised and gory,
  I joy to call Thee mine.

What Thou, my Lord, hast suffered
  Was all for sinners' gain;
Mine, mine was the transgression,
  But Thine the deadly pain;
Lo, here I fall, my Saviour!
  'Tis I deserve Thy place;
Look on me with Thy favor,
  Vouchsafe to me Thy grace.

What language shall I borrow
  To thank Thee, dearest Friend,
For this Thy dying sorrow,
  Thy pity without end?
Oh, make me Thine forever;
  And should I fainting be,
Lord, let me never, never
  Outlive my love to Thee!

Be near me when I'm dying;
  Oh, show Thy Cross to me!
And for my succor flying;
  Come, Lord, and set me free!
These eyes, new faith receiving,
  From Jesus shall not move;
For he who dies believing,
  Dies safely, through Thy love.

—BERNARD OF CLAIRVAUX, 1091-1153
  *Tr.* PAUL GERHARDT, 1607-1676

*English tr.*, JAMES WADDELL ALEXANDER,
  1859-1904

## ¶ NOT ALL THE BLOOD OF BEASTS

Not all the blood of beasts,
  On Jewish altars slain,
Could give the guilty conscience peace,
  Or wash away the stain.

But Christ, the heavenly Lamb,
  Takes all our sins away;
A sacrifice of nobler name,
  And richer blood than they.

34

My faith would lay her hand
  On that dear head of Thine,
While like a penitent I stand,
  And there confess my sin.

My soul looks back, to see
  The burdens Thou didst bear,
When hanging on the cursed tree,
  And hopes her guilt was there.

Believing, we rejoice
  To see the curse remove;
We bless the Lamb with cheerful voice,
  And sing His bleeding love.

—Isaac Watts, 1674-1748

35

# Penitential Reflections on Our Sins

### ¶ MY SINS, MY SAVIOUR!

My sins, my sins, my Saviour!
   They take such hold on me,
I am not able to look up,
   Save only Christ to Thee;
In Thee is all forgiveness,
   In Thee abundant grace,
My shadow and my sunshine
   The brightness of Thy face.

My sins, my sins, my Saviour!
   How sad on Thee they fall;
Seen through Thy gentle patience,
   I ten-fold feel them all;
I know they are forgiven,
   But still, their pain to me
Is all the grief and anguish
   They laid, my Lord, on Thee.

My sins, my sins, my Saviour!
   Their guilt I never knew
Till with Thee in the desert
   I near Thy passion drew;
Till with Thee in the garden
   I heard Thy pleading pray'r,
And saw the sweat-drops bloody
   That told Thy sorrow there.

36

Therefore my songs, my Saviour,
  E'en in this time of woe,
Shall tell of all Thy goodness
  To suffering man below;
Thy goodness and Thy favor,
  Whose presence from above
Rejoice those hearts my Saviour,
  That live in Thee alone.

—JOHN S. B. MONSELL, 1811-1875


## ¶ HAVE MERCY, GOD MOST HIGH

Have mercy on us, God Most High!
  Who lift our hearts to Thee;
Have mercy on us worms of earth,
  Most holy Trinity!

Most ancient of all mysteries!
  Before Thy throne we lie;
Have mercy now most merciful,
  Most holy Trinity!

When heaven and earth were yet unmade,
  When time was yet unknown,
Thou in Thy bliss and majesty
  Didst live and love alone!

Thou wert not born; there was no fount
  From which Thy Being flowed;
There is no end which Thou canst reach:
  But Thou art simply God.

How wonderful creation is,
  The work that Thou didst bless,
And, oh! what then must Thou be like,
  Eternal Loveliness?

37

How beautiful the Angels are,
　　The Saints how bright in bliss;
But with Thy beauty, Lord! compared,
　　How dull, how poor is this!

No wonder Saints have died of love,
　　No wonder hearts can break,
Pure hearts that once have learned to love
　　God for His own dear sake.

O listen, then, Most Pitiful!
　　To Thy poor creature's heart;
It blesses Thee that Thou art God,
　　That Thou art what Thou art!

Most ancient of all mysteries!
　　Still at Thy throne we lie;
Have mercy now, most merciful,
　　Most holy Trinity!

　　　　　—Frederick William Faber, 1814-1863


## ¶ O LORD, I AM ASHAMED TO SEEK THY FACE

O Lord, I am ashamed to seek Thy Face
　　As tho' I loved Thee as Thy saints love Thee:
　　Yet turn from those Thy lovers, look on me,
Disgrace me not with uttermost disgrace;
But pour on me ungracious, pour Thy grace
　　To purge my heart and bid my will go free,
　　Till I too taste Thy hidden Sweetness, see
Thy hidden Beauty in the holy place.
O Thou Who callest sinners to repent,
　　Call me Thy sinner unto penitence,
　　　For many sins grant me the greater love:
　　Set me above the waterfloods, above
Devil and shifting world and fleshly sense,
Thy Mercy's all-amazing monument.

　　　　　—Christina Rossetti, 1830-1894

# ¶ SCOURGE, BUT RECEIVE ME

Good Lord, today
I scarce find breath to say:
   Scourge, but receive me.
For stripes are hard to bear, but worse
Thy intolerable curse;
   So do not leave me.

Good Lord, lean down
In pity, tho' Thou frown;
   Smite, but retrieve me:
For so Thou hold me up to stand
And kiss Thy smiting hand,
   It less will grieve me.

—CHRISTINA ROSSETTI, 1830-1894

# Rejoicing in Forgiveness and Justification

¶ SONG OF ASSURANCE

Now I have found the ground wherein
  Sure my soul's anchor may remain,
The wounds of Jesus, for my sin
  Before the world's foundation slain;
Whose mercy shall unshaken stay,
When heaven and earth are fled away.

Father, Thine everlasting grace
  Our scanty thought surpasses far:
Thy heart still melts with tenderness.
  Thy arms of love still open are,
Returning sinners to receive,
That mercy they may taste and live.

O Love, Thou bottomless abyss,
  My sins are swallowed up in Thee!
Covered is my unrighteousness,
  Nor spot of guilt remains on me,
While Jesus' blood, through earth and skies,
Mercy, free, boundless mercy, cries.

With faith I plunge me in this sea;
  Here is my hope, my joy, my rest;
Hither, when hell assails, I flee,
  I look into my Saviour's breast;
Away, sad doubt, and anxious fear!
Mercy is all that's written there.

Though waves and storms go o'er my head,
  Though strength, and health, and friends
    be gone,
Though joys be withered all and dead,
  Though every comfort be withdrawn,
On this my steadfast soul relies, —
Father, Thy mercy never dies.

Fixed on this ground will I remain,
  Though my heart fail, and flesh decay;
This anchor shall my soul sustain,
  When earth's foundations melt away;
Mercy's full power I then shall prove,
Loved with an everlasting love.

—JOHANN ANDREAS ROTHE, 1688-1758
*Tr.* JOHN WESLEY, 1703-1791


## ¶ A GOOD CONFESSION

The chains that have bound me are flung to
    the wind,
  By the mercy of God the poor slave is set
    free;
And the strong grace of heaven breathes fresh
    o'er the mind,
  Like the bright winds of summer that glad-
    den the sea.

There was nought in God's world half so dark
    or so vile
  As the sin and the bondage that fettered
    my soul;
There was nought half so base as the malice
    and guile
  Of my own sordid passions, or Satan's con-
    trol.

41

For years I have borne about hell in my
      breast;
    When I thought of my God it was nothing
      but gloom;
Day brought me no pleasure, night gave me
      no rest,
    There was still the grim shadow of horrible
      doom.

It seemed as if nothing less likely could be
    Than that light should break in on a dun-
      geon so deep;
To create a new world were less hard than to
      free
    The slave from his bondage, the soul from
      its sleep.

But the word had gone forth, and said, Let
      there be light,
    And it flashed through my soul like a sharp
      passing smart;
One look to my Saviour, and all the dark night,
    Like a dream scarce remembered, was gone
      from my heart.

I cried out for mercy, and fell on my knees,
    And confessed, while my heart with keen
      sorrow was wrung;
'Twas the labor of minutes, and years of
      disease
    Fell as fast from my soul as the words from
      my tongue.
And now, blest be God and the sweet Lord
      who died!
    No deer on the mountain, no bird in the sky
No bright wave that leaps on the dark bound-
      ing tide,
    Is a creature so free or so happy as I.

All hail, then, all hail, to the dear Precious
    Blood,
  That hath worked these sweet wonders of
    mercy in me;
May each day countless numbers throng down
    to its flood,
  And God have His glory, and sinners go
    free.

—FREDERICK WILLIAM FABER, 1814-1863

## ¶ A SOUL IN ITS EARLIEST LOVE

O how happy are they
Who their Saviour obey,
And have laid up their treasure above;
  Tongue can never express
  The sweet comfort and peace
Of a soul in its earliest love.


That sweet comfort was mine,
When the favor divine
I received through the blood of the Lamb;
  When my heart first believed,
  What a joy I received—
What a heaven in Jesus' Name!


'Twas a heaven below
My Redeemer to know,
And the angels could do nothing more
  Than to fall at His feet,
  And the story repeat,
And the Lover of sinners adore.

Jesus all the day long
Was my joy and my song:
O that all His salvation might see;
   He hath loved me, I cried,
   He hath suffered and died,
To redeem even rebels like me.

   O the rapturous height
   Of that holy delight
Which I felt in the life-giving blood;
   Of my Saviour possessed,
   I was perfectly blessed
As if filled with the fulness of God.

—CHARLES WESLEY, 1707-1788

# Yearning for Purity of Heart

¶ I THIRST, THOU WOUNDED LAMB OF GOD

I thirst, Thou wounded Lamb of God,
To wash me in Thy cleansing blood;
To dwell within Thy wounds; then pain
Is sweet, and life or death is gain.

Take my poor heart, and let it be
Forever closed to all but Thee:
Seal Thou my breast, and let me wear
That pledge of love forever there.

How blest are they who still abide
Close shelter'd in Thy bleeding side!
Who thence their life and strength derive,
And by Thee move, and in Thee live.

What are our works but sin and death,
Till Thou thy quick'ning Spirit breathe?
Thou giv'st the power thy grace to move;
O wondrous grace! O boundless love!

How can it be, Thou heavenly King,
That Thou shouldst us to glory bring;
Make slaves the partners of thy throne,
Deck'd with a never-fading crown?

Hence our hearts melt, our eyes o'erflow,
Our words are lost, nor will we know,
Nor will we think of aught beside, —
My Lord, my Love is crucified.

—Attributed to JOHN WESLEY, 1703-1791


## ¶ PRAYER FOR PURITY

O Thou, to whose all-searching sight
The darkness shineth as the light,
Search, prove my heart; it pants for Thee;
O burst these bonds, and set it free!

Wash out its stains, refine its dross,
Nail my affections to the Cross;
Hallow each thought; let all within
Be clean, as Thou, my Lord, art clean!

If in this darksome wild I stray,
Be Thou my Light, be Thou my Way;
No foes, no violence I fear,
No fraud, while Thou, my God, art near.

When rising floods my soul o'erflow,
When sinks my heart in waves of woe,
Jesus, Thy timely aid impart,
And raise my head, and cheer my heart.

Saviour, where'er Thy steps I see,
Dauntless, untired, I follow Thee;
O let Thy hand support me still,
And lead me to Thy holy hill!

If rough and thorny be the way,
My strength proportion to my day;
Till toil, and grief, and pain shall cease,
Where all is calm, and joy, and peace.

—NICOLAUS LUDWIG VON ZINZENDORF,
1700-1760
*Tr.* JOHN WESLEY, 1703-1791


## JESUS, THINE ALL-VICTORIOUS LOVE

Jesus, thine all-victorious love
  Shed in my heart abroad:
Then shall my feet no longer rove,
  Rooted and fix'd in God.

O that in me the sacred fire
  Might now begin to glow;
Burn up the dross of base desire,
  And make the mountains flow.

O that it now from heaven might fall,
  And all my sins consume:
Come, Holy Ghost, for Thee I call;
  Spirit of burning, come.

Refining fire, go through my heart;
  Illuminate my soul;
Scatter Thy life through every part,
  And sanctify the whole.

My steadfast soul, from falling free,
  Shall then no longer move;
While Christ is all the world to me,
  And all my heart is love.

—CHARLES WESLEY, 1707-1788

# ¶ SELF-LOVE

Oh I could go through all life's troubles sing-
   ing,
   Turning earth's night to day,
If self were not so fast around me, clinging
   To all I do or say.


My very thoughts are selfish, always building
   Mean castles in the air;
I use my love of others for a gilding
   To make myself look fair.


I fancy all the world engrossed with judging
   My merit or my blame;
Its warmest praise seems an ungracious grudging
   Of praise which I might claim.


In youth or age, by city, wood, or mountain,
   Self is forgotten never;
Where'er we tread, it gushes like a fountain,
   And its waters flow for ever.


Alas! no speed in life can snatch us wholly
   Out of self's hateful sight;
And it keeps step, whene'er we travel slowly,
   And sleeps with us at night.


No grief's sharp knife, no pain's most cruel
      sawing
   Self and the soul can sever:
The surface, that in joy sometimes seems
      thawing,
   Soon freezes worse than ever.

Thus we are never men, self's wretched
 swathing
 Not letting virtue swell;
Thus is our whole life numbed, for ever
 bathing
 Within this frozen well.

O miserable omnipresence, stretching
 Over all time and space,
How have I run from thee, yet found thee
 reaching
 The goal in every race.

Inevitable self! vile imitation
 Of universal light, —
Within our hearts a dreadful usurpation
 Of God's exclusive right!

The opiate balms of grace may haply still
 thee,
 Deep in my nature lying;
For I may hardly hope, alas! to kill thee,
 Save by the act of dying.

O Lord! that I could waste my life for others,
 With no ends of my own,
That I could pour myself into my brothers,
 And live for them alone!

Such was the life Thou livedst; self-abjuring,
 Thine own pains never easing,
Our burdens bearing, our just doom enduring,
 A life without self-pleasing!

—Frederick William Faber, 1814-1863

49

# Aspirations After God

## ¶ AS PANTS THE HART

As pants the hart for cooling streams,
   When heated in the chase;
So longs my soul, O God, for Thee,
   And Thy refreshing grace.

For Thee, my God, the living God,
   My thirsty soul doth pine;
Oh, when shall I behold Thy face,
   Thou Majesty divine?

Why restless, why cast down, my soul?
   Trust God; who will employ
His aid for thee, and change these sighs
   To thankful hymns of joy.

God of my strength, how long shall I,
   Like one forgotten, mourn;
Forlorn, forsaken, and exposed
   To my oppressor's scorn?

I sigh to think of happier days,
   When Thou, O Lord! wast nigh;
When every heart was tuned to praise,
   And none more blessed than I.

Why restless, why cast down, my soul?
  Hope still; and thou shalt sing
The praise of Him who is Thy God,
  Thy health's eternal spring.

—NAHUM TATE, 1652-1715
—NICHOLAS BRADY, 1659-1726
Psalm 42 paraphrase

## ¶ THE WAY OF PERFECTION

Oh how the thought of God attracts
  And draws the heart from earth,
And sickens it of passing shows
  And dissipating mirth!

'Tis not enough to save our souls,
  To shun the eternal fires;
The thought of God will rouse the heart
  To more sublime desires.

God only is the creature's home,
  Though rough and straight the road;
Yet nothing less can satisfy
  The love that longs for God.

Oh utter but the Name of God
  Down in your heart of hearts,
And see how from the world at once
  All tempting light departs.

A trusting heart, a yearning eye,
  Can win their way above;
If mountains can be moved by faith,
  Is there less power in love?

How little of that road, my soul!
  How little hast thou gone!
Take heart, and let the thought of God
  Allure thee further on.

The freedom from all wilful sin,
  The Christian's daily task, —
Oh these are graces far below
  What longing love would ask!

Dole not thy duties out to God,
  But let thy hand be free:
Look long at Jesus; His sweet Blood,
  How was it dealt to thee?

The perfect way is hard to flesh;
  It is not hard to love;
If thou wert sick for want of God,
  How swiftly wouldst thou move!

Then keep thy conscience sensitive;
  No inward token miss:
And go where grace entices thee; —
  Perfection lies in this.

Be docile to thine unseen Guide,
  Love Him as He loves thee;
Time and obedience are enough,
  And thou a saint shall be.

—FREDERICK WILLIAM FABER, 1814-1863


¶ THOU SHEPHERD OF ISRAEL, AND MINE

Thou Shepherd of Israel, and mine,
  The joy and desire of my heart,
For closer communion I pine;
  I long to reside where Thou art:

The pasture I languish to find,
  Where all, who their Shepherd obey,
Are fed, on Thy bosom reclined,
  And screen'd from the heat of the day.

'Tis there, with the lambs of Thy flock,
  There only, I covet to rest;
To lie at the foot of the rock,
  Or rise to be hid in Thy breast:
'Tis there I would always abide,
  And never a moment depart, —
Conceal'd in the cleft of Thy side,
  Eternally held in Thy heart.

—CHARLES WESLEY, 1707-1788


¶ THE FERVOR OF HOLY DESIRE

  Still, still, without ceasing,
  I feel it increasing,
This fervor of holy desire;
  And often exclaim,
  Let me die in the flame
Of a love that can never expire!

  Had I words to explain,
  What she must sustain,
Who dies to the world and its ways;
  How joy and affright,
  Distress and delight,
Alternately checker her days;

  Thou, sweetly severe!
  I would make thee appear,
In all thou art pleas'd to award,
  Not more in the sweet,
  Than the bitter I meet,
My tender and merciful Lord.

53

This Faith, in the dark
Pursuing its mark,
Through many sharp trials of Love,
Is the sorrowful waste,
That is to be pass'd,
In the way to the Canaan above.

—JEANNE MARIE DE LA MOTTE-GUYON,
1648-1717
*Tr.* Unknown


¶ DESIRE OF GOD

Oh for freedom, for freedom in worshipping
God,
For the mountain-top feeling of generous
souls,
For the health, for the air, of the hearts deep
and broad,
Where  grace not in rills but in cataracts rolls!

Most good is the brisk wholesome service of
fear,
And the calm wise obedience of conscience is
sweet;
And good are all worships, all loyalties dear,
All promptitudes fitting, all services meet.

But none honours God like the thirst of desire,
Nor possesses the heart so completely with
Him;
For it burns the world out with the swift ease
of fire,
And fills life with good works till it runs o'er
the brim.

Then pray for desire, for love's wistfullest
    yearning,
For the beautiful pining of holy desire;
Yes, pray for a soul that is ceaselessly burn-
    ing
With the soft fragrant flames of this thrice
    happy fire.

For the heart only dwells, truly dwells with
    its treasure,
And the languor of love captive hearts can
    unfetter;
And they who love God cannot love Him by
    measure,
For their love is but hunger to love Him still
    better.

Is it hard to serve God, timid soul? Hast
    thou found
Gloomy forests, dark glens, mountain-tops on
    thy way?
All the hard would be easy, all the tangles
    unwound,
Wouldst thou only desire, as well as obey.

For the lack of desire is the ill of all ills;
Many thousands through it the dark pathway
    have trod,
The balsam, the wine of predestinate wills
Is a jubilant pining and longing for God.

'Tis a fire that will burn what thou canst not
    pass over;
'Tis a lightning that breaks away all bars to
    love;
'Tis a sunbeam the secrets of God to discover;
'Tis the wing David prayed for, the wing of the
    Dove.

I have seen living men—and their good angels
    know
How they failed and fell short through the
    want of desire:
Souls once almost saints have descended so
    low,
'Twill be much if their wings bear them over
    the fire.

I have seen dying men not so grand in their
    dying
As our love would have wished,—and through
    lack of desire:
Oh that we may die languishing, burning, and
    sighing;
For God's last grace and best is to die all
    on fire.

'Tis a great gift of God to live after our Lord,
Yet the old Hebrew times they were ages of
    fire.
When fainting souls fed on each dim figured
    word,
And God called men He loved most—the Men
    of Desire.

Oh then wish more for God, burn more with
    desire,
Covet more the dear sight of his marvellous
    Face;
Pray louder, pray longer, for the sweet gift of
    fire
To come down on thy heart with its whirl-
    winds of grace.

Yes, pine for thy God, fainting soul! ever
    pine;
Oh languish mid all that life brings thee of
    mirth;
Famished, thirsty, and restless, —let such life
    be thine,—
For what sight is to heaven, desire is to earth.

God loves to be longed for, He loves to be
    sought,
For He sought us Himself with such longing
    and love:
He died for desire of us, marvellous thought!
And He yearns for us now to be with Him
    above.

—FREDERICK WILLIAM FABER, 1814-1863

## ¶ SATISFIED

Draw me to Thee, till far within Thy rest,
In stillness of Thy peace, Thy voice I hear—
For ever quieted upon Thy breast,
    So loved, so near.

By mystery of Thy touch my spirit thrilled,
    O Magnet all Divine;
The hunger of my soul for ever stilled,
    For Thou art mine.

For me, O Lord, the world is all too small,
    For I have seen Thy face,
Where Thine eternal love irradiates all
    Within Thy secret place.
And therefore from all others, from all else,
    Draw Thou my soul to Thee . . .
. . . Yea—Thou hast broken the enchanter's spells,
    And I am free.

Now in the haven of untroubled rest
    I land at last,
The hunger, and the thirst, and weary quest
    For ever past.
There, Lord, to lose, in bliss of Thine embrace
    The recreant will;
There, in the radiance of Thy blessed Face,
    Be hushed and still;
There, speechless at Thy pierced Feet
    See none and nought beside,
And know but this—that Thou art sweet,
    That I am satisfied.

—GERHARD TERSTEEGEN, 1697-1769
*Tr.* Unknown

# Delighting in God's Presence

¶ GOD IS PRESENT EVERYWHERE

They who seek the throne of grace
Find that throne in every place;
If we live a life of prayer,
God is present everywhere.

In our sickness and our health,
In our want, or in our wealth,
If we look to God in prayer,
God is present everywhere.

When our earthly comforts fail,
When the woes of life prevail,
'Tis the time for earnest prayer;
God is present everywhere.

Then, my soul, in every strait,
To thy Father come, and wait;
He will answer every prayer:
God is present everywhere.

—OLIVER HOLDEN, 1765-1844


¶ THE ROYAL PRIESTHOOD

The race of God's anointed priests
    Shall never pass away;
Before His glorious face they stand,
    And serve Him night and day.

59

Though reason raves, and unbelief
  Flows on, a mighty flood,
There are, and shall be till the end,
  The hidden priests of God.

His chosen souls, their earthly dross
  Consumed in sacred fire,
To God's own heart their hearts ascend
  In flame of deep desire;
The incense of their worship fills
  His Temple's holiest place;
Their song with wonder fills the Heavens,
  The glad new song of grace.

—GERHARD TERSTEEGEN, 1697-1769
*Tr.* Unknown

¶ GOD REVEALS HIS PRESENCE

God reveals His presence:
Let us now adore Him,
And with awe appear before Him.
  God is in His temple:
  All within keep silence,
Prostrate lie with deepest reverence.
    Him alone
    God we own,
  Him our God and Saviour:
  Praise His Name for ever!

God reveals His presence:
Hear the harps resounding;
See the crowds the throne surrounding;
  "Holy, holy, holy!"
  Hear the hymn ascending,

60

Angels, saints, their voices blending.
> Bow Thine ear
> To us here;
Hearken, O Lord Jesus,
To our meaner praises.

O Thou Fount of blessing
Purify my spirit,
Trusting only in Thy merit:
> Like the holy angels
> Who behold Thy glory,
May I ceaselessly adore Thee.
> Let Thy will
> Ever still
Rule Thy Church terrestrial,
As the hosts celestial.

—GERHARD TERSTEEGEN, 1697-1769
Composite translation

# ¶ WITHIN THE HOLY PLACE

His priest am I, before Him day and night,
> Within His Holy Place;
And death, and life, and all things dark and bright,
> I spread before His Face.
Rejoicing with His joy, yet ever still,
> For silence is my song;
My work to bend beneath His blessed will,
> All day, and all night long—
For ever holding with Him converse sweet,
Yet speechless, for my gladness is complete.

—GERHARD TERSTEEGEN, 1697-1769
*Tr.* Unknown

# ¶ LO, GOD IS HERE!

Lo, God is here! let us adore,
  And own how dreadful is this place;
Let all within us feel His power,
  And silent bow before His face;
Who know His power, His grace who prove,
Serve Him with awe, with reverence love.

Lo, God is here! Him day and night
  United choirs of angels sing;
To Him, enthroned above all height,
  Heaven's host their noblest praises bring;
Disdain not, Lord, our meaner song,
Who praise Thee with a stammering tongue.

Being of beings, may our praise
  Thy courts with grateful fragrance fill;
Still may we stand before Thy face,
  Still hear and do Thy sovereign will;
To Thee may all our thoughts arise,
Ceaseless, accepted sacrifice.

—GERHARD TERSTEEGEN, 1697-1769
*Tr.* JOHN WESLEY, 1703-1791


# ¶ ALLURED INTO THE DESERT

Allured into the desert,
  With God alone, apart,
There spirit meeteth spirit,
  There speaketh heart to heart.
Far, far on that untrodden shore,
  God's secret place I find;
Alone I pass the golden door,
  The dearest left behind.

62

There God and I—none other;
  Oh far from men to be!
Nay, midst the crowd and tumult,
  Still, Lord, alone with Thee.
Still folded close upon Thy breast,
  In field, and mart, and street,
Untroubled in that perfect rest,
  That isolation sweet.

O God, Thou art far other
  Than men have dreamed and taught,
Unspoken in all language,
  Unpictured in all thought.
Thou God art God—he only learns
  What that great Name must be,
Whose raptured heart within him burns,
  Because he walks with Thee.

Stilled by that wondrous Presence,
  That tenderest embrace,
The years of longing over,
  Do we behold Thy Face;
We seek no more than Thou hast given,
  We ask no vision fair,
Thy precious Blood has opened Heaven,
  And we have found Thee there.

O weary souls, draw near Him;
  To you I can but bring
One drop of that great ocean,
  One blossom of that spring;
Sealed with His kiss, my lips are dumb,
  My soul with awe is still;
Let him that is athirst but come,
  And freely drink his fill.

              —GERHARD TERSTEEGEN, 1697-1769
              *Tr.* Unknown

              63

# The Raptures of Divine Love

### ¶ O LOVE DIVINE!

O Love Divine! that stoop'st to share
  Our sharpest pang, our bitterest tear,
On Thee we cast each earth-born care,
  We smile at pain while Thou art near.


Though long the weary way we tread,
  And sorrow crown each lingering year,
No path we shun, no darkness dread,
  Our hearts still whispering, "Thou art near."


When drooping pleasure turns to grief,
  And trembling faith is changed to fear,
The murmuring wind, the quivering leaf,
  Shall softly tell us Thou art near.


On Thee we cast our burdening woe,
  O Love Divine, for ever dear;
Content to suffer while we know,
  Living or dying, Thou art near!

—OLIVER WENDELL HOLMES, 1809-1894

## ¶ I LOVE MY GOD

I love my God, but with no love of mine,
    For I have none to give;
I love thee, Lord; but all the love is Thine,
    For by Thy life I live.
I am as nothing, and rejoice to be
Emptied, and lost, and swallowed up in Thee.

Thou, Lord, alone, art all Thy children need,
    And there is none beside;
From Thee the streams of blessedness proceed
    In Thee the blest abide, —
Fountain of life, and all-abounding grace,
Our source, our center, and our dwelling-place.

>               —JEANNE MARIE DE LA MOTTE-GUYON,
>               1648-1717
>               *Tr.* Unknown


## ¶ THE ACQUIESCENCE OF PURE LOVE

Love! if thy destined sacrifice am I,
Come, slay thy victim, and prepare Thy fires;
Plunged in Thy depths of mercy, let me die
The death which every soul that lives desires.

I watch my hours, and see them fleet away;
The time is long that I have languished here;
Yet all my thoughts Thy purposes obey,
With no reluctance, cheerful and sincere.

To me 'tis equal, whether Love ordain
My life or death, appoint me pain or ease;
My soul perceives no real ill in pain;
In ease or health no real good she sees.

One good she covets, and that good alone,
To choose Thy will, from selfish bias free;
And to prefer a cottage to a throne,
And grief to comfort, if it pleases Thee.

That we should bear the cross is Thy command,
Die to the world, and live to self no more;
Suffer, unmoved, beneath the rudest hand;
When shipwrecked pleased as when upon the shore.

> —JEANNE MARIE DE LA MOTTE-GUYON,
> 1648-1717
> *Tr.* Unknown

## ¶ JESUS, THY BOUNDLESS LOVE TO ME

Jesus, Thy boundless love to me
   No thought can reach, no tongue declare;
O knit my thankful heart to Thee,
   And reign without a rival there:
Thine wholly, Thine alone I am:
Be Thou alone my constant flame.

O grant that nothing in my soul
   May dwell, but Thy pure love alone;
O may Thy love possess me whole,
   My joy, my treasure, and my crown:
Strange fires far from my soul remove;
May every act, word, thought, be love.

O Love, how cheering is Thy ray;
   All pain before Thy presence flies;
Care, anguish, sorrow, melt away,
   Where'er Thy healing beams arise;
O Jesus, nothing may I see,
Nothing desire, or seek, but Thee.

In suffering, be Thy love my peace;
  In weakness, be Thy love my power;
And, when the storms of life shall cease,
  Jesus, in that important hour,
In death, as life, be Thou my guide,
And save me, who for me hast died.

—PAUL GERHARDT, 1607-1676
*Tr.* John Wesley, 1703-1791

## ¶ O LOVE DIVINE!

O Love divine, how sweet Thou art!
When shall I find my willing heart
  All taken up by Thee?
I thirst, I faint, I die to prove
The greatness of redeeming love,—
  The love of Christ to me.

Stronger His love than death or hell;
Its riches are unsearchable;
  The first-born sons of light
Desire in vain its depths to see;
They cannot reach the mystery,
  The length, the breadth, the height.

God only knows the love of God;
O that it now were shed abroad
  In this poor stony heart:
For love I sigh, for love I pine;
This only portion, Lord, be mine;
  Be mine this better part.

O that I could forever sit
With Mary at the Master's feet!
  Be this my happy choice;
My only care, delight, and bliss,
My joy, my heaven on earth, be this,
  To hear the Bridegroom's voice.

O that I could, with favor'd John,
Recline my weary head upon
   The dear Redeemer's breast:
From care, and sin, and sorrow free,
Give me, O Lord, to find in Thee
   My everlasting rest.

—Charles Wesley, 1707-1788


## ¶ THE HIDDEN LOVE OF GOD

Thou hidden Love of God, whose height,
   Whose depth unfathomed, no man knows,
I see from far Thy beauteous light,
   Inly I sigh for Thy repose;
My heart is pained, nor can it be
At rest till it finds rest in Thee.

Thy secret voice invites me still
   The sweetness of Thy yoke to prove;
And fain I would; but, though my will
   Seem fixed, yet wide my passions rove.
Yet hindrances strew all the way;
I aim at Thee, yet from Thee stray.

'Tis mercy all, that Thou hast brought
   My mind to seek her peace in Thee;
Yet, while I seek but find Thee not,
   No peace my wandering soul shall see.
O when shall all my wanderings end,
And all my steps to Thee-ward tend?

Is there a thing beneath the sun
   That strives with Thee my heart to share?

Ah! tear it thence, and reign alone,
   The Lord of every motion there;
Then shall my heart from earth be free,
When it hath found repose in Thee.

—GERHARD TERSTEEGEN, 1697-1769<br>
Tr. John Wesley, 1703-1791


## ¶ LOVE'S IMMENSITY

   O past and gone!
How great is God! how small am I!
A mote in the illimitable sky,
Amidst the glory deep, and wide, and high
   Of Heaven's unclouded sun.
There to forget myself for evermore;
Lost, swallowed up in Love's immensity,
The sea that knows no sounding and no shore,
   God only there, not I.

More near than I unto myself can be,
   Art Thou to me;
So have I lost myself in finding Thee,
Have lost myself for ever, O my Sun!
The boundless Heaven of Thine eternal love
Around me, and beneath me, and above;
  In glory of that golden day
  The former things are passed away—
   I, past and gone.

—GERHARD TERSTEEGEN, 1697-1769<br>
Tr. Unknown

# The Rest of Faith

¶ ALL MUST BE WELL

Through the love of God our Saviour,
    All will be well;
Free and changeless is His favor,
    All, all is well;
Precious is the blood that heal'd us,
Perfect is the grace that seal'd us,
Strong the hand stretch'd out to shield us,
    All must be well.

Though we pass through tribulation,
    All will be well;
Ours is such a full salvation,
    All, all is well;
Happy, still in God confiding,
Fruitful, if in Christ abiding
Holy, through the Spirit's guiding,
    All must be well.

We expect a bright tomorrow,
    All will be well;
Faith can sing, through days of sorrow,
    All, all is well;
On our Father's love relying,
Jesus ev'ry need supplying,
Or in living or in dying,
    All must be well.

—MARY BOWLEY PETERS, 1813-1856

# ¶ CONFIDENCE

If thou but suffer God to guide thee,
  And hope in Him through all thy ways,
He'll give thee strength, whate'er betide thee,
  And bear thee through the evil days;
Who trusts in God's unchanging love
Builds on the rock that nought can move.

What can these anxious cares avail thee,
  These never-ceasing moans and sighs?
What can it help if thou bewail thee
  O'er each dark moment as it flies?
Our cross and trials do but press
The heavier for our bitterness.

Only be still, and wait His leisure
  In cheerful hope, with heart content
To take whate'er thy Father's pleasure
  And all-discerning love hath sent;
Nor doubt our inmost wants are known
To Him who chose us for His own.

Sing, pray, and keep His ways unswerving;
  So do thine own part faithfully,
And trust His word,—though undeserving,
  Thou yet shalt find it true for thee;
God never yet forsook at need
The soul that trusted Him indeed.

—George C. Neumark, 1621-1681
*Tr.* Catherine Winkworth, 1829-1878


# ¶ SOMETIMES A LIGHT SURPRISES

Sometimes a light surprises
  The Christian while he sings;
It is the Lord, who rises
  With healing in His wings:

71

When comforts are declining,
  He grants the soul again
A season of clear shining,
  To cheer it after rain.

In holy contemplation,
  We sweetly then pursue
The theme of God's salvation,
  And find it ever new:
Set free from present sorrow,
  We cheerfully can say,
"E'en let the unknown morrow
  Bring with it what it may."

It can bring with it nothing,
  But He will bear us through;
Who gives the lilies clothing,
  Will clothe His people too:
Beneath the spreading heavens,
  No creature but is fed;
And He who feeds the ravens
  Will give His children bread.

—WILLIAM COWPER, 1731-1800

## ¶ THE BLESSED JOURNEY

Let Him lead thee blindfold onwards,
  Love needs not to know;
Children whom the Father leadeth
  Ask not where they go.
Though the path be all unknown,
Over moors and mountains lone.

72

Give no ear to reason's questions;
　　Let the blind man hold
That the sun is but a fable
　　Men believed of old.
At the breast the babe will grow;
Whence the milk he need not know.

—GERHARD TERSTEEGEN, 1697-1769
*Tr.* Unknown

## ¶ JESUS, I AM RESTING, RESTING

Jesus, I am resting, resting
　　In the joy of what Thou art,
I am finding out the greatness
　　Of Thy loving heart.
Here I gaze and gaze upon Thee,
　　As Thy beauty fills my soul,
For by Thy transforming power,
　　Thou hast made me whole.

O how great Thy loving-kindness,
　　Vaster, broader than the sea;
O how marvellous Thy goodness
　　Lavished all on me—
Yes, I rest in Thee, Beloved,
　　Know what wealth of grace is Thine,
Know Thy certainty of promise
　　And have made it mine.

Simply trusting Thee, Lord Jesus,
　　I behold Thee as Thou art,
And Thy love, so pure, so changeless,
　　Satisfies my heart,

Satisfies its deepest longing,
Meets, supplies my every need,
Compasseth me round with blessings:
Thine is love indeed.

Ever lift Thy face upon me
As I work and wait for Thee;
Resting 'neath Thy smile, Lord Jesus,
Earth's dark shadows flee.
Brightness of my Father's glory,
Sunshine of my Father's face,
Let Thy glory e'er shine on me,
Fill me with Thy grace.

—JEAN SOPHIA PIGOTT, 19th Century


## ¶ RESIGNATION

A little bird I am,
Shut from the fields of air;
And in my cage I sit and sing
To Him who placed me there;
Well pleased a prisoner to be,
Because, my God, it pleases Thee.

Naught have I else to do;
I sing the whole day long;
And He whom most I love to please
Doth listen to my song;
He caught and bound my wandering wing,
But still He bends to hear me sing.

Thou hast an ear to hear,
A heart to love and bless;
And though my notes were e'er so rude,
Thou wouldst not hear the less;
Because Thou knowest, as they fall,
That love, sweet love, inspires them all.

My cage confines me round;
　　Abroad I cannot fly;
But though my wing is closely bound,
　　My heart's at liberty.
My prison walls cannot control
The flight, the freedom, of the soul.

O, it is good to soar
　　These bolts and bars above,
To Him whose purpose I adore,
　　Whose providence I love;
And in Thy mighty will to find
The joy, the freedom, of the mind.

　　　　　　　—JEANNE MARIE DE LA MOTTE-GUYON,
　　　　　　　1648-1717
　　　　　　　*Tr.* Unknown


¶ IN HEAVENLY LOVE ABIDING

In heavenly love abiding,
　　No change my heart shall fear;
And safe is such confiding,
　　For nothing changes here:
The storm may roar without me,
　　My heart may low be laid;
But God is round about me,
　　And can I be dismayed?

Wherever He may guide me,
　　No want shall turn me back;
My Shepherd is beside me,
　　And nothing can I lack.
His wisdom ever waketh,
　　His sight is never dim:
He knows the way He taketh,
　　And I will walk with Him.

Green pastures are before me,
  Which yet I have not seen;
Bright skies will soon be o'er me,
  Where the dark clouds have been.
My hope I cannot measure:
  My path to life is free:
My Saviour has my treasure,
  And He will walk with me.

—ANNA LAETITIA WARING, 1820-1910


¶ THE REMEMBRANCE OF MERCY

Why art thou sorrowful, servant of God?
  And what is this dullness that hangs o'er
    thee now?
Sing the praises of Jesus, and sing them
    aloud,
  And the song shall dispel the dark cloud
    from thy brow.

For is there a thought in the wide world so
    sweet,
  As that God has so cared for us, bad as
    we are,
That He thinks of us, plans for us, stoops to
    entreat,
  And follows us, wander we ever so far?

Then how can the heart e'er be drooping or
    sad,
  Which God hath once touched with the
    light of His grace?
Can the child have a doubt who but lately
    hath laid
  Himself to repose in his father's embrace?

76

And is it not wonderful, servant of God!
  That He should have honoured us so with
    His love,
That the sorrows of life should but shorten
    the road
  Which leads to Himself and the mansion
    above?

Oh then when the spirit of darkness comes
    down
  With clouds and uncertainties into thy
    heart,
One look to thy Saviour, one thought of thy
    crown,
  And the tempest is over, the shadows de-
    part.

That God hath once whispered a word in
    thine ear,
  Or sent thee from heaven one sorrow for
    sin,
Is enough for a life both to banish all fear,
  And to turn into peace all the troubles
    within.

The schoolmen can teach thee far less
    about heaven,
  Of the height of God's power, or the depth
    of His love,
Than the fire in thy heart when thy sin was
    forgiven,
  Or the light that one mercy brings down
    from above.

Then why dost thou weep so? For see how
    time flies,
  The time that for loving and praising was
    given!

Away with thee, child, then, and hide thy red
   eyes
In the lap, the kind lap, of thy Father in
   heaven.

—FREDERICK WILLIAM FABER, 1814-1863

# The Spiritual Warfare

¶ DISTRACTIONS IN PRAYER

Ah dearest Lord! I cannot pray,
  My fancy is not free;
Unmannerly distractions come,
  And force my thoughts from Thee.

The world that looks so dull all day
  Glows bright on me at prayer,
And plans that ask no thought but then
  Wake up and meet me there.

All nature one full fountain seems
  Of dreamy sight and sound,
Which, when I kneel, breaks up its deeps,
  And makes a deluge round.

Old voices murmur in my ear,
  New hopes start to life,
And past and future gaily blend
  In one bewitching strife.

My very flesh has restless fits;
  My changeful limbs conspire
With all these phantoms of the mind
  My inner self to tire.

I cannot pray; yet, Lord! Thou knowst
    The pain it is to me
To have my vainly struggling thoughts
    Thus torn away from Thee.

Sweet Jesus! teach me how to prize
    These tedious hours when I,
Foolish and mute before Thy Face,
    In helpless worship lie.

Prayer was not meant for luxury,
    Or selfish pastime sweet;
It is the prostrate creature's place
    At his Creator's Feet.

Had I, dear Lord! no pleasure found
    But in the thought of Thee,
Prayer would have come unsought, and been
    A truer liberty.

Yet Thou art oft most present, Lord!
    In weak distracted prayer:
A sinner out of heart with self
    Most often finds Thee there.

For prayer that humbles sets the soul
    From all illusions free,
And teaches it how utterly,
    Dear Lord! it hangs on Thee.

The heart, that on self-sacrifice
    Is covetously bent,
Will bless Thy chastening hand that makes
    Its prayer its punishment.

My Saviour! why should I complain
    And why fear aught but sin?
Distractions are but outward things;
    Thy peace dwells far within.

These surface-troubles come and go,
  Like rufflings of the sea;
The deeper depth is out of reach
  To all, my God, but Thee.

—FREDERICK WILLIAM FABER, 1814-1863


## ¶ THE BENEFITS OF SUFFERING

By sufferings only can we know
  The nature of the life we live;
The temper of our souls they show,
  How true, how pure, the love we give.
To leave my love in doubt would be
No less disgrace than misery!

I welcome, then, with heart sincere,
  The cross my Saviour bids me take;
No load, no trial, is severe,
  That's borne or suffered for His sake:
And thus my sorrow shall proclaim
A love that's worthy of the name.

—JEANNE MARIE DE LA MOTTE-GUYON,
1648-1717
*Tr.* Unknown


## ¶ SORROW AND LOVE

Self-love no grace in sorrow sees,
Consults her own peculiar ease,
  'Tis all the bliss she knows;
But nobler aims true Love employ,
In self-denial is her joy,
  In suffering her repose.

81

Sorrow and Love go side by side;
Nor height nor depth can e'er divide
    Their heaven-appointed bands;
Those dear associates still are one,
Nor, till the race of life is run,
    Disjoin their wedded hands.

Thy choice and mine shall be the same,
Inspirer of that holy flame,
    Which must forever blaze!
To take the cross and follow Thee,
Where love and duty lead, shall be
    My portion and my praise.

> —JEANNE MARIE DE LA MOTTE-GUYON,
> 1648-1717
> *Tr.* Unknown

# Victory Through Praise

## ¶ COME, O MY SOUL

Come, O my soul, in sacred lays,
Attempt thy great Creator's praise:
But, oh, what tongue can speak His fame!
What mortal verse can reach the theme!

Enthroned amid the radiant spheres,
He glory like a garment wears;
To form a robe of light divine,
Ten thousand suns around Him shine.

In all our Maker's grand designs,
Omnipotence, with wisdom, shines;
His works, through all this wondrous frame,
Declare the glory of His Name.

Raised on devotion's lofty wing,
Do thou, my soul, His glories sing;
And let His praise employ thy tongue,
Till listening worlds shall join the song!

—THOMAS BLACKLOCK, 18th Century

83

## ¶ BLESS, O MY SOUL, THE LIVING GOD

Bless, O my soul, the living God,
Call home thy thoughts that rove abroad;
Let all the pow'rs within me join
In work and worship so divine.

Bless, O my soul, the God of grace;
His favors claim thy highest praise;
Why should the wonders He hath wrought
Be lost in silence, and forgot?

'Tis He, my soul, that sent His Son
To die for crimes which thou hast done;
He owns the ransom, and forgives
The hourly follies of our lives.

Let the whole earth His power confess,
Let the whole earth adore His grace;
The Gentile with the Jew shall join
In work and worship so divine.

—Isaac Watts, 1674-1748
After Psalm 103


## ¶ I'LL PRAISE MY MAKER

I'll praise my Maker while I've breath,
And when my voice is lost in death,
    Praise shall employ my nobler powers;
My days of praise shall ne'er be past,
While life, and thought, and being last,
    Or immortality endures.

Happy the man whose hopes rely
On Israel's God; He made the sky,
  And earth, and seas, with all their train;
His truth for ever stands secure,
He saves the opprest, He feeds the poor,
  And none shall find His promise vain.

The Lord pours eyesight on the blind;
The Lord supports the fainting mind;
  He sends the labouring conscience peace;
He helps the stranger in distress,
The widow and the fatherless,
  And grants the prisoner sweet release.

I'll praise Him while He lends me breath,
And when my voice is lost in death,
  Praise shall employ my nobler powers;
My days of praise shall ne'er be past,
While life, and thought, and being last,
  Or immortality endures.

    —ISAAC WATTS, 1674-1748
    *Al.* John Wesley, 1703-1791


¶ I SING TH' ALMIGHTY POWER OF GOD

I sing th' almighty power of God,
  That made the mountains rise,
That spread the flowing seas abroad,
  And built the lofty skies.

I sing the wisdom that ordained
  The sun to rule the day;
The moon shines full at His command,
  And all the stars obey.

85

I sing the goodness of the Lord,
    That filled the earth with food;
He formed the creatures with His word,
    And then pronounced them good.

Lord! how Thy wonders are displayed
    Where'er I turn mine eye!
If I survey the ground I tread,
    Or gaze upon the sky!

There's not a plant or flower below
    But makes Thy glories known;
And clouds arise, and tempests blow,
    By order from Thy throne.

Creatures that borrow life from Thee
    Are subject to Thy care;
There's not a place where we can flee
    But God is present there.

—ISAAC WATTS, 1674-1748


¶ NOW THANK WE ALL OUR GOD

Now thank we all our God,
With heart, and hands, and voices,
    Who wondrous things hath done,
In whom His world rejoices;
    Who from our mother's arms
        Hath blessed us on our way
    With countless gifts of love,
        And still is ours today.

O may this bounteous God
Through all our life be near us,
  With ever joyful hearts
And blessed peace to cheer us;
  And keep us in His grace,
    And guide us when perplexed,
  And free us from all ills
    In this world and the next.


  All praise and thanks to God
The Father now be given,
  The Son, and Him who reigns
With them in highest heaven,
  The one eternal God,
    Whom earth and heaven adore;
  For thus it was, is now,
    And shall be evermore.

—MARTIN RINCKART, 1586-1649
*Tr.* Catharine Winkworth, 1829-1878


## ¶ TE DEUM LAUDAMUS

We praise Thee, O God,
  we acknowledge Thee to be the Lord.
All the earth doth worship Thee,
  the Father everlasting.
To Thee all angels cry aloud,
  the heavens and all the powers therein;
To Thee Cherubim and Seraphim
  continually do cry,
Holy, holy, holy, Lord God of Sabaoth:
Heaven and earth are full of the majesty
  of Thy glory.

The glorious company of the Apostles
    praise Thee.
The goodly fellowship of the Prophets
    praise Thee.
The noble army of Martyrs praise Thee.
The holy Church throughout all the world
    doth acknowledge Thee,
The Father of an infinite Majesty;
Thine adorable, true and only Son;
Also the Holy Ghost, the Comforter.


Thou art the King of Glory, O Christ;
Thou art the everlasting Son of the Father.
When Thou tookest upon Thee to deliver man
Thou didst humble Thyself
    to be born of a virgin.
When Thou hadst overcome the sharpness of death
Thou didst open the kingdom of heaven
    to all believers.
Thou sittest at the right hand of God
    in the glory of the Father.
We believe that Thou shalt come
    to be our Judge.
We therefore pray Thee help Thy servants
    whom Thou hast redeemed
    with Thy precious blood.
Make them to be numbered with Thy saints
    in glory everlasting.


O Lord, save Thy people,
    and bless Thine heritage.
Govern them, and lift them up forever.
Day by day we magnify Thee,
And we worship Thy Name forever,
    world without end.
Vouchsafe, O Lord, to keep us
    this day without sin.

O Lord, have mercy upon us,
  have mercy upon us.
O Lord, let Thy mercy be upon us,
  as our trust is in Thee.
O Lord, in Thee have I trusted,
  let me never be confounded.

# The Prayer of Quiet

## ¶ THE SPIRIT OF PRAYER

The prayers I make will then be sweet indeed
If Thou the Spirit give by which I pray:
My unassisted heart is barren clay,
That of its native self can nothing feed:
Of good and pious works Thou art the seed,
That quickens only where Thou say'st it may:
Unless Thou show to us Thine own true way
No man can find it: Father! Thou must lead.
Do Thou, then, breathe those thoughts into my mind
By which such virtue may in me be bred
That in Thy holy footsteps I may tread;
The fetters of my tongue do Thou unbind,
That I may have the power to sing of Thee,
And sound Thy praises everlastingly.

> —From the Italian of Michael Angelo,
> 1475-1564
> *Tr.* William Wordsworth, 1770-1850

## ¶ MY GOD! SILENT TO THEE!

As, down in the sunless retreats of the ocean,
   Sweet flowers are springing no mortal can see,
So, deep in my heart, the still prayer of devotion,
   Unheard by the world, rises, silent, to Thee,
      My God! silent, to Thee,—
      Pure, warm, silent, to Thee.

As still to the star of its worship, though clouded,
  The needle points faithfully o'er the dim sea,
So, dark as I roam, thro' this wintry world shrouded,
  The hope of my spirit turns, trembling, to Thee,
    My God! trembling, to Thee,—
    True, fond, trembling, to Thee.

—THOMAS MOORE, 1719-1852


## ¶ GOD'S ETERNAL NOW

Stillness midst the ever-changing,
  Lord, my rest art Thou;
So for me has dawned the morning,
  God's eternal NOW.
Now for me the day unsetting,
  Now the song begun;
Now, the deep surpassing glory,
  Brighter than the sun.

Hail! all hail! thou peaceful country
  Of eternal calm;
Summer land of milk and honey,
  Where the streams are balm.
There the Lord my Shepherd leads me,
  Wheresoe'er He will;
In the fresh green pastures feeds me,
  By the waters still.

Well I know them, those still waters!
  Peace and rest at last;
In their depths the quiet heavens
  Tell the storms are past,
Nought to mar the picture fair,
Of the glory resting there.

—GERHARD TERSTEEGEN, 1697-1769
*Tr.* Unknown

91

# ¶ MY HEART IS RESTING, O MY GOD

My heart is resting, O my God,
   I will give thanks and sing;
My heart is at the secret source
   Of every precious thing.
Now the frail vessel Thou hast made
   No hand but Thine shall fill;
For the waters of the earth have failed,
   And I am thirsty still.

I thirst for springs of heavenly life,
   And here all day they rise;
I seek the treasure of Thy love,
   And close at hand it lies.
And a new song is in my mouth
   To long-loved music set:
"Glory to Thee for all the grace
   I have not tasted yet;

"Glory to Thee for strength withheld,
   For want and weakness known;
And the fear that sends me to Thy breast
   For what is most my own."
I have a heritage of joy
   That yet I must not see;
But the hand that bled to make it mine
   Is keeping it for me.

My heart is resting, O my God,
   My heart is in Thy care;
I hear the voice of joy and health
   Resounding everywhere.
"Thou art my portion," saith my soul,
   Ten thousand voices say,
And the music of their glad Amen
   Will never die away.

—ANNA LAETITIA WARING, 1820-1910

## ¶ HIDDEN IN GOD'S HEART

How good it is, when weaned from all beside,
With God alone the soul is satisfied,
    Deep hidden in His heart!
How good it is, redeemed, and washed, and shriven,
To dwell, a cloistered soul, with Christ in heaven,
    Joined, never more to part!

How good the heart's still chamber thus to close
    On all but God alone—
There in the sweetness of His love repose,
    His love unknown!
All else for ever lost—forgotten all
    That else can be;
In rapture undisturbed, O Lord, to fall
    And worship Thee.

No place, no time, 'neath those eternal skies—
How still, how sweet, and how surpassing fair
That solitude in glades of Paradise,
And, as in olden days, God walking there.
I hear His voice amidst the stillness blest,
    And care and fear are past—
I lay me down within His arms to rest
    From all my works at last.

How good it is when from the distant land,
From lonely wanderings, and from weary ways,
The soul hath reached at last the golden strand,
    The Gates of Praise!
There, where the tide of endless love flows free,
    There, in the sweet and glad eternity,
    The still, unfading Now.
Ere yet the days and nights of earth are o'er,
Begun the day that is for evermore—
    Such rest art Thou!

        —GERHARD TERSTEEGEN, 1697-1769
        *Tr.* Unknown

# The Bliss of Communion

¶ THE DISCIPLE TO HIS LORD

Teach me to do the thing that pleaseth Thee;
  Thou art my God, in Thee I live and move;
Oh, let Thy loving Spirit lead me forth
  Into the land of righteousness and love.

Thy love the law and impulse of my soul,
  Thy righteousness its fitness and its plea,
Thy loving Spirit mercy's sweet control
  To make me liker, draw me nearer Thee.

My highest hope to be where, Lord, Thou art,
  To lose myself in Thee my richest gain,
To do Thy will the habit of my heart,
  To grieve the Spirit my severest pain.

Thy smile my sunshine, all my peace from thence,
  From self alone what could that peace destroy?
Thy joy my sorrow at the least offence,
  My sorrow that I am not more Thy joy.

—JOHN S. B. MONSELL, 1811-1875


¶ JOY IN THE PRESENCE OF JESUS

How tedious and tasteless the hours
  When Jesus no longer I see!
Sweet prospects, sweet birds, and sweet flowers,
  Have all lost their sweetness to me;—

The midsummer sun shines but dim,
  The fields strive in vain to look gay;
But when I am happy in Him,
  December's as pleasant as May.

His Name yields the richest perfume,
  And sweeter than music His voice;
His presence disperses my gloom,
  And makes all within me rejoice;
I should, were He always thus nigh,
  Have nothing to wish or to fear;
No mortal so happy as I,
  My summer would last all the year.

Content with beholding His face,
  My all to His pleasure resign'd,
No changes of season or place
  Would make any change in my mind:
While blest with a sense of His love,
  A palace a toy would appear;
And prisons would palaces prove,
  If Jesus would dwell with me there.

My Lord, if indeed I am Thine,
  If Thou art my sun and my song,
Say, why do I languish and pine?
  And why are my winters so long?
O drive these dark clouds from my sky;
  Thy soul-cheering presence restore;
Or take me to Thee up on high,
  Where winter and clouds are no more.

—John Newton, 1725-1807


¶ O JESUS, KING MOST WONDERFUL

O Jesus, King most wonderful,
  Thou Conqueror renowned,
Thou Sweetness most ineffable,
  In whom all joys are found!

When once Thou visitest the heart,
　　Then truth begins to shine,
Then earthly vanities depart,
　　Then kindles love divine.

O Jesus, Light of all below!
　　Thou Fount of life and fire!
Surpassing all the joys we know,
　　And all we can desire,—

May every heart confess Thy Name,
　　And ever Thee adore,
And, seeking Thee, itself inflame
　　To seek Thee more and more.

Thee may our tongues for ever bless,
　　Thee may we love alone,
And ever in our lives express
　　The image of Thine own.

　　　　—BERNARD OF CLAIRVAUX, 1091-1153
　　　　*Tr.* Edward Caswall, 1814-1878


## ¶ CHRIST OUR LIGHT

O Christ our Light, Whom even in darkness we
　(So we look up) discern and gaze upon,
　O Christ, Thou loveliest Light that ever shone,
Thou Light of Light, Fount of all lights that be,
Grant us clear vision of Thy Light to see,
　Tho' other lights elude us, or begone
　Into the secret of oblivion,
Or gleam in places higher than man's degree.
Who looks on Thee looks full on his desire
　Who looks on Thee looks full on Very Love:
　　Looking, he answers well, "What lack I yet?"
His heat and cold wait not on earthly fire,
　His wealth is not of earth to lose or get;
　Earth reels, but he has stored his store above.

　　　　—CHRISTINA ROSSETTI, 1830-1894

# ¶ AS OINTMENT POURED FORTH

Is this that Name as ointment poured forth
  For which the virgins love Thee; King of kings
  And Lord of lords? All seraphs clad in wings;
All Cherubs and all Wheels which south and north,
Which east and west turn not in going forth;
  All many-semblanced ordered spirits, as rings
  Of rainbow in unwonted fashionings,
Might answer, Yes. But we from south and north,
From east and west, a feeble folk who came
  By desert ways in quest of land unseen,
  A promised land of pasture ever green
    And ever springing ever singing wave,
Know best Thy Name of Jesus: Blessed Name,
  Man's life and resurrection from the grave.

—CHRISTINA ROSSETTI, 1830-1894


# ¶ O! TELL ME, THOU LIFE AND
# DELIGHT OF MY SOUL!

O! tell me, Thou life and delight of my soul,
  Where the flock of Thy pastures are feeding;
I seek Thy protection, I need Thy control,
  I would go where my Shepherd is leading.

O! tell me the place where Thy flocks are at rest,
  Where the noontide will find them reposing?
The tempest now rages, my soul is distress'd,
  And the pathway of peace I am losing.

O! why should I stray with the flocks of Thy foes,
  'Mid the desert where now they are roving,
Where hunger and thirst, where affliction and woes,
  And temptations their ruin are proving!

O! when shall my foes and my wandering cease?
 And the follies that fill me with weeping!
Thou Shepherd of Israel, restore me that peace
 Thou dost give to the flock Thou art keeping.

A voice from the Shepherd now bids thee return
 By the way where the footprints are lying:
No longer to wander, no longer to mourn;
 O fair one, now homeward be flying!

—THOMAS HASTINGS, 1784-1872


## ¶ THE FACE OF CHRIST

A rose, a lily, and the Face of Christ
 Have all our hearts sufficed:
For He is Rose of Sharon nobly born,
 Our Rose without a thorn;
And He is Lily of the Valley, He
 Most sweet in purity.
But when we come to name Him as He is,
 Godhead, Perfection, Bliss,
All tongues fall silent, while pure hearts alone
 Complete their orison.

—CHRISTINA ROSSETTI, 1830-1894


## ¶ CHRIST, WHOSE GLORY FILLS THE SKIES

Christ, whose glory fills the skies,
 Christ, the true, the only light,
Sun of Righteousness, arise!
 Triumph o'er the shades of night;
Day-spring from on high, be near!
Day-star, in my heart appear!

Dark and cheerless is the morn,
　If Thy life is hid from me;
Joyless is the day's return,
　Till Thy mercy's beams I see;
Till they inward light impart,
Warmth and gladness to my heart.

Visit, then, this soul of mine;
　Pierce the gloom of sin and grief;
Fill me, radiant Sun divine;
　Scatter all my unbelief;
More and more Thyself display,
Shining to the perfect day.

　　　　—CHARLES WESLEY, 1707-1788


## ¶ JESU, HIGHEST HEAVEN'S COMPLETENESS

Jesu, highest heaven's completeness,
　Name of music to the ear,
To the lips surpassing sweetness,
　Wine the fainting heart to cheer.

Eating Thee, the soul may hunger,
　Drinking, still athirst may be;
But for earthly food no longer,
　Nor for any stream but Thee.

Jesu, all delight exceeding,
　Only hope of heart distrest;
Weeping eyes and spirit mourning
　Find in Thee a place of rest.

Stay, O Beauty uncreated,
　Ever ancient, ever new;
Banish deeds of darkness hated,
　With Thy sweetness all bedew.

99

Jesu, fairest blossom springing
From a maiden ever pure,
May our lips Thy praise be singing
While eternal years endure.

—BERNARD OF CLAIRVAUX, 1091-1153
*Tr.* Robert Campbell, 1814-1868


## ¶ SHOW ME THY FACE

Show me Thy face—one transient gleam
  Of loveliness divine,
And I shall never think or dream
  Of other love save Thine:
All lesser light will darken quite,
  All lower glories wane,
The beautiful of earth will scarce
  Seem beautiful again.

Show me Thy face—my faith and love
  Shall henceforth fixed be,
And nothing here have power to move
  My soul's serenity.
My life shall seem a trance, a dream,
  And all I feel and see,
Illusive, visionary—Thou
  The one reality!

Show me Thy face—I shall forget
  The weary days of yore,
The fretting ghosts of vain regret
  Shall haunt my soul no more.
All doubts and fears for future years
  In quiet trust subside,
And naught but blest content and calm
  Within my breast abide.

100

Show me Thy face—the heaviest cross
  Will then seem light to bear;
There will be gain in every loss,
  And peace with every care.
With such light feet the years will fleet,
  Life seem as brief as blest,
Till I have laid my burden down,
  And entered into rest.

—AUTHOR UNKNOWN


## ¶ NONE OTHER LAMB, NONE OTHER NAME

None other Lamb, none other Name,
  None other Hope in heaven or earth or sea,
None other Hiding-place from guilt and shame,
  None beside Thee.

My faith burns low, my hope burns low;
  Only my heart's desire cries out in me,
By the deep thunder of its want and woe,
  Cries out to Thee.

Lord, Thou art Life, though I be dead;
  Love's Fire Thou art, however cold I be:
Nor heaven have I, nor place to lay my head,
  Nor home, but Thee.

—CHRISTINA ROSSETTI, 1830-1894


## ¶ ASPIRATIONS OF THE SOUL AFTER CHRIST

My Spouse! in whose presence I live,
  Sole object of all my desires,
Who know'st what a flame I conceive,
  And canst easily double its fires;

101

How pleasant is all that I meet!
  From fear of adversity free,
I find even sorrow made sweet,
  Because 'tis assign'd me by Thee.

Transported I see Thee display
  Thy riches and glory divine;
I have only my life to repay,
  Take what I would gladly resign.
Thy will is the treasure I seek,
  For Thou art as faithful as strong;
There let me, obedient and meek,
  Repose myself all the day long.

My spirit and faculties fail;
  Oh finish what Love has begun!
Destroy what is sinful and frail,
  And dwell in the soul Thou hast won!
Dear theme of my wonder and praise,
  I cry, who is worthy as Thou!
I can only be silent and gaze;
  'Tis all that is left to me now.

Oh glory, in which I am lost,
  Too deep for the plummet of thought!
On an ocean of Deity toss'd,
  I am swallow'd, I sink into nought.
Yet lost and absorb'd as I seem,
  I chant to the praise of my King;
And though overwhelm'd by the theme,
  Am happy whenever I sing.

—JEANNE MARIE DE LA MOTTE-GUYON,
1648-1718
*Tr.* Unknown

# ¶ THE PAIN OF LOVE

Jesus! why dost Thou love me so?
   What hast Thou seen in me
To make my happiness so great,
   So dear a joy to Thee?

Wert Thou not God, I then might think
   Thou hadst no eye to read
The badness of that selfish heart,
   For which Thine own did bleed.

But Thou art God, and knowest all;
   Dear Lord! Thou knowest me;
And yet Thy knowledge hinders not
   Thy love's sweet liberty.

Ah, how Thy grace hath wooed my soul
   With persevering wiles!
Now give me tears to weep; for tears
   Are deeper joy than smiles.

Each proof renewed of Thy great love
   Humbles me more and more,
And brings to light forgotten sins,
   And lays them at my door.

The more I love Thee, Lord! the more
   I hate my own cold heart;
The more Thou woundest me with love,
   The more I feel the smart.

What shall I do, then, dearest Lord!
   Say, shall I fly from Thee,
And hide my poor unloving self
   Where Thou canst never see?

Or shall I pray that Thy dear love
  To me might not be given?
Ah, no! love must be pain on earth,
  If it be bliss in heaven.

—FREDERICK WILLIAM FABER, 1814-1863


## ¶ THOU HIDDEN SOURCE OF CALM REPOSE

Thou hidden Source of calm repose,
  Thou all-sufficient Love Divine,
My help and refuge from my foes,
  Secure I am, if Thou art mine;
And lo! from sin, and grief, and shame,
I hide me, Jesus, in Thy Name.

Thy mighty Name salvation is,
  And keeps my happy soul above;
Comfort it brings, and power, and peace,
  And joy, and everlasting love;
To me, with Thy dear Name, are given
Pardon, and holiness, and heaven.

Jesus, my all in all Thou art;
  My rest in toil, my ease in pain,
The medicine of my broken heart;
  In war my peace, in loss my gain,
My smile beneath the tyrant's frown,
In shame my glory and my crown:

In want my plentiful supply,
  In weakness my almighty power;
In bonds my perfect liberty,
  My light in Satan's darkest hour;
My joy in grief, my shield in strife,
In death my everlasting life.

—CHARLES WESLEY, 1707-1788

# ¶ THE MAN DIVINE

In the Paradise of glory
  Is the Man Divine;
There my heart, O God, is tasting
  Fellowship with Thine.
Called to share Thy joy unmeasured,
  Now is heaven begun;
I rejoice with Thee, O Father,
  In Thy glorious Son.


Where the heart of God is resting,
  I have found my rest;
Christ who found me in the desert,
  Laid me on His breast.
There in deep unhindered fulness
  Doth my joy flow free—
On through everlasting ages,
  Lord, beholding Thee.


Round me is creation groaning,
  Death, and sin, and care;
But there is a rest remaining,
  And my Lord is there.
There I find a blessed stillness
  In His courts of love;
All below but strife and darkness,
  Cloudless peace above.


'Tis a solitary pathway
  To that fair retreat—
Where in deep and sweet communion
  Sit I at His feet.
In that glorious isolation,
  Loneliness how blest,
From the windy storm and tempest
  Have I found my rest.

Learning from Thy lips for ever
  All the Father's heart,
Thou hast, in that joy eternal,
  Chosen me my part.
There, where Jesus, Jesus only,
  Fills each heart and tongue,
Where Himself is all the radiance
  And Himself the song.

Here, who follows Him the nearest,
  Needs must walk alone;
There like many seas the chorus,
  Praise surrounds the throne.
Here a dark and silent pathway;
  In those courts so fair
Countless hosts, yet each beholding
  Jesus only, there.

—"T. P."


## ¶ THEE WILL I LOVE

Thee will I love, my Strength, my Tower,
  Thee will I love, my Joy, my Crown,
Thee will I love with all my power,
  In all Thy works, and Thee alone;
Thee will I love, till the pure fire
Fill my whole soul with chaste desire.

Ah, why did I so late Thee know,
  Thee, lovelier than the sons of men!
Ah, why did I no sooner go
  To Thee, the only ease in pain!
Ashamed, I sigh, and inly mourn,
That I so late to Thee did turn.

I thank Thee, uncreated Sun,
  That Thy bright beams on me have shined;
I thank Thee, who hast overthrown
  My foes, and healed my wounded mind;
I thank Thee, whose enlivening voice
Bids my freed heart in Thee rejoice.

Uphold me in the doubtful race,
  Nor suffer me again to stray;
Strengthen my feet with steady pace
  Still to press forward in Thy way;
My soul and flesh, O Lord of might,
Fill, satiate, with Thy heavenly light.

Give to mine eyes refreshing tears,
  Give to my heart chaste, hallowed fires,
Give to my soul, with filial fires,
  The love that all heaven's host inspires;
That all my powers, with all their might,
In Thy sole glory may unite.

Thee will I love, my Joy, my Crown,
  Thee will I love, my Lord, my God;
Thee will I love, beneath Thy frown,
  Or smile, Thy sceptre, or Thy rod;
What though my flesh and heart decay,
Thee shall I love in endless day.

—JOHANN SCHEFFLER, 1624-1677
Tr. John Wesley, 1703-1791

¶ AT THE LORD'S TABLE

Here, O my Lord, I see Thee face to face;
  Here would I touch and handle things unseen,
Here grasp with firmer hand the eternal grace,
  And all my weariness upon Thee lean.

Here would I feed upon the bread of God,
  Here drink with Thee the royal wine of heaven;
Here would I lay aside each earthly load,
  Here taste afresh the calm of sin forgiven.


This is the hour of banquet and of song;
  This is the heavenly table spread for me;
Here let me feast, and feasting, still prolong
  The brief bright hour of fellowship with Thee.


Too soon we rise; the symbols disappear;
  The feast, though not the love, is past and gone;
The bread and wine remove, but Thou art here,
  Nearer than ever; still my Shield and Sun.


I have no help but Thine; nor do I need
  Another arm save Thine to lean upon;
It is enough, my Lord, enough indeed;
  My strength is in Thy might, Thy might
    alone.


Mine is the sin, but Thine the righteousness;
  Mine is the guilt, but Thine the cleansing
    blood;
Here is my robe, my refuge, and my peace, —
  Thy blood, Thy righteousness, O Lord my
    God.


Feast after feast thus comes and passes by,
  Yet, passing, points to the glad feast above,
Giving sweet foretaste of the festal joy,
  The Lamb's great bridal feast of bliss and
    love.


—HORATIUS BONAR, 1808-1889

108

## ¶ PRAYER BEFORE COMMUNION

Bread of the world, in mercy broken,
　Wine of the soul, in mercy shed,
By whom the words of life were spoken,
　And in whose death our sins are dead:
Look on the heart by sorrow broken,
　Look on the tears by sinners shed;
And be Thy feast to us the token
　That by Thy grace our souls are fed.

　　　　—REGINALD HEBER, 1783-1826

## ¶ THE INDWELLING CHRIST

Thou who givest of Thy gladness
　　Till the cup runs o'er—
Cup whereof the pilgrim weary
　　Drinks to thirst no more—
Not a-nigh me, but within me
　　Is Thy joy divine;
Thou, O Lord, hast made Thy dwelling
　　In this heart of mine.

Need I that a law should bind me
　　Captive unto Thee?
Captive is my heart, rejoicing
　　Never to be free.
Ever with me, glorious, awful,
　　Tender, passing sweet,
One upon whose heart I rest me,
　　Worship at His Feet.

With me, wheresoe'er I wander,
　　That great Presence goes,
That unutterable gladness,
　　Undisturbed repose.

Everywhere the blessed stillness
  Of His Holy Place—
Stillness of the love that worships
  Dumb before His Face.

To Thy house, O God my Father,
  Thy lost child is come;
Led by wandering lights no longer,
  I have found my home.
Over moor and fen I tracked them
  Through the midnight blast,
But to find the Light eternal
  In my heart at last.

—GERHARD TERSTEEGEN, 1697-1769
*Tr.* Unknown

## ¶ AS INCENSE STREAMING FORTH

Thy Name, O Christ, as incense streaming forth
  Sweetens our names before God's Holy Face;
Luring us from the south and from the north
  Unto the sacred place.

In Thee God's promise is Amen and Yea.
  What art Thou to us? Prize of every lot,
Shepherd and Door, our Life and Truth and Way:—
  Nay, Lord, what art Thou not?

—CHRISTINA ROSSETTI, 1830-1894

## ¶ HOSANNA, LORD!

Hosanna to the living Lord!
Hosanna to th' incarnate Word!
To Christ, Creator, Saviour, King,
Let earth, let heaven, Hosanna sing!

Hosanna, Lord! Thine angels cry;
Hosanna, Lord! Thy saints reply;
Above, beneath us, and around,
The dead and living swell the sound.

O Saviour, with protecting care,
Return to this Thy house of prayer:
Where we Thy parting promise claim:
Assembled in Thy sacred Name.

But, chiefest, in our cleansèd breast,
Eternal! bid Thy Spirit rest;
And make our secret soul to be
A temple pure, and worthy Thee.

So in the last and dreadful day,
When earth and heaven shall melt away,
Thy flock, redeemed from sinful stain,
Shall swell the sound of praise again.

—REGINALD HEBER, 1783-1826

## ¶ AM I NOT ENOUGH?

Am I not enough, Mine own? enough,
     Mine own, for thee?
Hath the world its palace towers,
Garden glades of magic flowers,
   Where thou fain wouldst be?
Fair things and false are there,
False things but fair.
  All shalt thou find at last,
     Only in Me.
Am I not enough, Mine own? I, for ever
  and alone, I, needing thee?

—GERHARD TERSTEEGEN, 1697-1769
*Tr.* Unknown

111

# ¶ JESUS, THOU JOY OF LOVING HEARTS

Jesus, Thou Joy of loving hearts,
   Thou Fount of life, Thou Light of men,
From the best bliss that earth imparts
   We turn unfilled to Thee again.

Thy truth unchanged hath ever stood;
   Thou savest those that on Thee call:
To them that seek Thee Thou art good,
   To them that find Thee, all in all.

We taste Thee, O Thou living Bread,
   And long to feast upon Thee still;
We drink of Thee, the Fountain-head,
   And thirst our souls from Thee to fill.

Our restless spirits yearn for Thee,
   Where'er our changeful lot is cast, —
Glad when Thy gracious smile we see,
   Blest when our faith can hold Thee fast.

O Jesus, ever with us stay;
   Make all our moments calm and bright;
Chase the dark night of sin away;
   Shed o'er the world Thy holy light.

          —BERNARD OF CLAIRVAUX, 1091-1153
          *Tr.* Ray Palmer, 1808-1887

# Joyous Anticipation of Christ's Return

## ¶ WAKE, AWAKE, FOR NIGHT IS FLYING

"Wake, awake, for night is flying,"
The watchmen on the heights are crying;
 "Awake, Jerusalem, at last!"
Midnight hears the welcome voices,
And at the thrilling cry rejoices:
 "Come forth, ye virgins, night is past!
The Bride-groom comes, awake,
Your lamps with gladness take;
 Hallelujah!
And for His marriage feast prepare,
For ye must go to meet Him there."


Zion hears the watchmen singing,
And all her heart with joy is springing;
 She wakes, she rises from her gloom;
For her Lord comes down all glorious,
The strong in grace, in truth victorious,
 Her Star is risen, her Light is come!
Ah come, Thou blessèd Lord,
O Jesus, Son of God,
 Hallelujah!
We follow till the halls we see
Where Thou hast bid us sup with Thee.

113

Now let all the heavens adore Thee,
And men and angels sing before Thee,
    With harp and cymbal's clearest tone;
Of one pearl each shining portal,
Where we are with the choir immortal
    Of angels round Thy dazzling throne;
Nor eye hath seen, nor ear
Hath yet attained to hear,
    What there is ours;
But we rejoice, and sing to Thee
Our hymns of joy eternally.

—Philipp Nicolai, 1556-1608
Tr. Catherine Winkworth, 1829-1878

¶ LO! HE COMES!

Lo! He comes, with clouds descending,
    Once for favored sinners slain:
Thousand thousand saints attending,
    Swell the triumph of His train:
        Hallelujah!
God appears on earth to reign!

See the universe in motion,
    Sinking on her funeral pyre—
Earth dissolving, and the ocean
    Vanishing in final fire:
        Hark the trumpet!
Loud proclaims the Day of Ire!

Graves have yawned in countless numbers,
    From the dust the dead arise;
Millions out of silent slumbers,
    Wake in overwhelmed surprise;
        Where creation
Wrecked and torn on ruin lies!

114

See the Judge our nature wearing,
   Pure, ineffable, divine:
See the great Archangel bearing
   High in heaven the mystic sign:
      Cross of Glory!
Christ be in that moment mine!


Every eye shall now behold Him
   Robed in dreadful majesty;
Those who set aside and sold Him,
   Pierced and nailed Him to the tree,
      Deeply wailing,
Shall the true Messiah see.


All the tokens of His passion
   Still His dazzling body bears;
Cause of endless exultation
   To His ransomed worshippers;
      With what rapture
Gaze we on those glorious scars.


Lo! the last long separation!
   As the cleaving crowds divide;
And one dread adjudication
   Sends each soul to either side!
      Lord of mercy!
How shall I that day abide!


O, may Thine own Bride and Spirit
   Then avert a dreadful doom,
And me summon to inherit
   An eternal blissful home:—
      Ah! come quickly!
Let Thy second advent come!

Yea, Amen! Let all adore Thee
  High on Thine eternal throne!
Saviour—take the power and glory;
  Make Thy righteous sentence known:
    Jah! Jehovah!
Claim the kingdom for Thine own.

> —JOHN CENNICK, *et al.* 1718-1755

## ¶ THE HOPE OF HIS COMING

There is a balm for every pain,
  A medicine for all sorrow;
The eye turned backward to the Cross,
  And forward to the morrow.

The morrow of the glory and the psalm,
    When He shall come;
The morrow of the harping and the palm,
    The welcome home.
Meantime in His beloved hands our ways,
And on His Heart the wandering heart at rest;
And comfort for the weary one who lays
    His head upon His Breast.

> —GERHARD TERSTEEGEN, 1697-1769
> *Tr.* Unknown

## ¶ THE BLESSED MORROW

'Midst the darkness, storm, and sorrow,
  One bright gleam I see;
Well I know the blessed morrow
  Christ will come for me.
'Midst the light, and peace, and glory
  Of the Father's home,
Christ for me is watching, waiting,
  Waiting till I come.

Long the blessed Guide has led me
  By the desert road;
Now I see the golden towers,
  City of my God.
There, amidst the love and glory,
  He is waiting yet;
On His hands a name is graven
  He can ne'er forget.


There, amidst the songs of heaven,
  Sweeter to His ear
Is the footfall through the desert,
  Ever drawing near.
There, made ready are the mansions,
  Radiant, still, and fair;
But the Bride the Father gave Him
  Yet is wanting there.


Who is this who comes to meet me
  On the desert way,
As the Morning Star foretelling
  God's unclouded day?
He it is who came to win me
  On the Cross of shame;
In His glory well I know Him
  Evermore the same.


Oh the blessed joy of meeting,
  All the desert past!
Oh the wondrous words of greeting
  He shall speak at last!
He and I together entering
  Those fair courts above—
He and I together sharing
  All the Father's love.

Where no shade nor stain can enter,
  Nor the gold be dim,
In that holiness unsullied,
  I shall walk with Him.
Meet companion then for Jesus,
  From Him, for Him, made—
Glory of God's grace for ever
  There in me displayed.

He who in His hour of sorrow
  Bore the curse alone;
I who through the lonely desert
  Trod where He had gone;
He and I, in that bright glory,
  One deep joy shall share—
Mine, to be for ever with Him;
  His, that I am there.

  —GERHARD TERSTEEGEN, 1697-1769
  *Tr.* Unknown

# Immortality and the World to Come

Lift your glad voices in triumph on high,
For Jesus hath risen, and man cannot die.
Vain were the terrors that gathered around Him,
  And short the dominion of death and the grave;
He burst from the fetters of darkness that bound Him,
  Resplendent in glory, to live and to save.
Loud was the chorus of angels on high, —
  "The Saviour hath risen, and man shall not die."


Glory to God, in full anthems of joy;
The being He gave us, death cannot destroy.
Sad were the life we must part with tomorrow,
  If tears were our birthright, and death were our end;
But Jesus hath cheered the dark valley of sorrow,
  And bade us, immortal, to heaven ascend.
Lift, then, your voices in triumph on high,
For Jesus hath risen, and man shall not die.

—HENRY WARE, 1794-1843

119

# ¶ JESUS LIVES, AND SO SHALL I

Jesus lives, and so shall I.
   Death! thy sting is gone forever:
He, who deigned for me to die,
   Lives, the bands of death to sever.
He shall raise me with the just:
Jesus is my Hope and Trust.

Jesus lives and reigns supreme;
   And, His kingdom still remaining,
I shall also be with Him,
   Ever living, ever reigning.
God has promised; be it must:
Jesus is my Hope and Trust.

Jesus lives, and God extends
   Grace to each returning sinner;
Rebels He receives as friends,
   And exalts to highest honor.
God is True as He is Just;
Jesus is my Hope and Trust.

Jesus lives, and by His grace,
   Victory o'er my passions giving,
I will cleanse my heart and ways,
   Ever to His glory living.
The weak He raises from the dust:
Jesus is my Hope and Trust.

Jesus lives, and I am sure
   Naught shall e'er from Jesus sever,
Satan's wiles, and Satan's power,
   Pain or pleasure—ye shall never!
Christian armor can not rust:
Jesus is my Hope and Trust.

Jesus lives, and death is now
But my entrance into glory.
Courage! then, my soul, for thou
Hast a crown of life before thee;
Thou shalt find thy hopes were just—
Jesus is the Christian's Trust.

—Christian F. Gellert, 1715-1769
*Tr.* Unknown


## ¶ O SING HALLELUJAH!

Our Lord Christ hath risen!
The tempter is foiled;
His legions are scattered,
His strongholds are spoiled.
O sing Hallelujah! O sing Hallelujah!
O sing Hallelujah, be joyful and sing,
Our great foe is baffled—Christ Jesus is King!

O sin, thou art vanquished,
Thy long reign is o'er;
Though still thou dost vex us,
We dread thee no more.
O sing Hallelujah! O sing Hallelujah!
O sing Hallelujah, be joyful and sing,
Who now can condemn us? Christ Jesus is King!

O death we defy thee!
A stronger than thou
Hath entered thy palace;
We fear thee not now!
O sing Hallelujah! O sing Hallelujah!
O sing Hallelujah, be joyful and sing,
The grave cannot scare us—Christ Jesus is King!